PRESENTED TO:

GIVEN BY:

A SPECIAL NOTE:

INSTANT INSPIRATION for Your BUSY LIFE

1 MINUTE DAILY DEVOTIONS

ISBN 978-1-60587-534-7

Published by Freeman-Smith, a division of Worthy Media, Inc.,
134 Franklin Road, Suite 200, Brentwood, Tennessee 37027.

The quoted ideas expressed in this book (but not Scripture verses) are not, in all cases, exact quotations, as some have been edited for clarity and brevity. In all cases, the author has attempted to maintain the speaker's original intent. In some cases, quoted material for this book was obtained from secondary sources, primarily print media. While every effort was made to ensure the accuracy of these sources, the accuracy cannot be guaranteed. For additions, deletions, corrections, or clarifications in future editions of this text, please write Freeman-Smith.

Cover Design by Kim Russell / Wahoo Designs
Page Layout by Bart Dawson

Printed in the United States of America

1 2 3 4 5—CHG—17 16 15 14 13

INSTANT INSPIRATION for Your BUSY LIFE

1 MINUTE DAILY DEVOTIONS

FS
FREEMAN-SMITH

Introduction

Can you spare one minute each day for God? Of course you can . . . and of course you should! No matter how busy you are, you should never allow the temptations and distractions of everyday living to distance you from your Creator.

This world offers limitless opportunities to stray from the path that God intends for your life. You are confronted with temptations and distractions that were unknown to previous generations. And, the world is changing so rapidly that, at times, it seems difficult to catch your breath and keep your balance. This book is intended to help. It contains 150 short devotional readings for people who, like you, are busily engaged in life.

The ideas on these pages will encourage you to give God your undivided attention for at least one minute each day. But make no mistake: the emphasis in the previous sentence should be placed on the words "at least." In truth, you can, and should, give God significantly more time than that. And when you do so, you'll be rewarded.

Do you have questions that you can't answer? Are you seeking to change some aspect of your life? Do you want to be a better person and a better Christian? If so, ask for God's help, starting with a regular time of devotional reading and prayer. Even one minute is enough time to change your day . . . and your life.

Finding Time for God

Every morning he wakes me. He teaches me to listen like a student. The Lord God helps me learn...

Isaiah 50:4-5 NCV

Each new day is a gift from God, and if we are wise, we will spend a few quiet moments each morning thanking the Giver. Daily life is woven together with the threads of habit, and no habit is more important to our spiritual health than the discipline of daily prayer and devotion to the Creator.

When we begin each day with heads bowed and hearts lifted, we remind ourselves of God's love, His protection, and His commandments. And if we are wise, we align our priorities for the coming day with the teachings and commandments that God has given us through His Holy Word.

Are you seeking to change some aspect of your life? Do you seek to improve the condition of your spiritual, physical, or emotional health? If so, ask for God's help and ask for it many times each day . . . starting with your morning devotional.

Our devotion to God is strengthened when we offer Him a fresh commitment each day.

Elizabeth George

God First

Honor GOD with everything you own; give him the first and the best. Your barns will burst, your wine vats will brim over.

Proverbs 3:9-10 MSG

As you think about the nature of your relationship with God, remember this: you will always have some type of relationship with Him—it is inevitable that your life must be lived in relationship to God. The question is not if you will have a relationship with Him; the burning question is whether that relationship will be one that seeks to honor Him . . . or not.

Are you willing to place God first in your life? And, are you willing to welcome God's Son into your heart? Unless you can honestly answer these questions with a resounding yes, then your relationship with God isn't what it could be or should be. Thankfully, God is always available, He's always ready to forgive, and He's waiting to hear from you now. The rest, of course, is up to you.

God deserves first place in your life . . . and you deserve the experience of putting Him there.

Jim Gallery

Christ's Love

Just as the Father has loved Me, I also have loved you. Remain in My love.

John 15:9 HCSB

How much does Christ love us? More than we, as mere mortals, can comprehend. His love is perfect and steadfast. Even though we are fallible and wayward, the Good Shepherd cares for us still. Even though we have fallen far short of the Father's commandments, Christ loves us with a power and depth that is beyond our understanding. The sacrifice that Jesus made upon the cross was made for each of us, and His love endures to the edge of eternity and beyond.

Christ's love changes everything. When you accept His gift of grace, you are transformed, not only for today, but also for all eternity. If you haven't already done so, accept Jesus Christ as your Savior. He's waiting patiently for you to invite Him into your heart. Please don't make Him wait a single minute longer.

Live your lives in love, the same sort of love which Christ gives us, and which He perfectly expressed when He gave Himself as a sacrifice to God.

Corrie ten Boom

Prayer Changes Things

And everything—whatever you ask in prayer, believing—you will receive.

Matthew 21:22 HCSB

Is prayer an integral part of your daily life, or is it a hit-or-miss habit? Do you "pray without ceasing," or is your prayer life an afterthought? As you consider the role that prayer currently plays in your life—and the role that you think it should play—remember that the quality of your spiritual life is inevitably related to the quality of your prayer life.

Prayer changes things and it changes you. So today, instead of turning things over in your mind, turn them over to God in prayer. Instead of worrying about your next decision, pray about it. Don't limit your prayers to meals or to bedtime. Pray often about things great and small. God is listening, and He wants to hear from you. Now.

Prayer isn't just preparation for the battle; prayer is the battle.

Bob Logan

Making Time for God

Happy are those who hear the joyful call to worship, for they will walk in the light of your presence, Lord.

Psalm 89:15 NLT

Are you making time each day to praise God and to study His Word? If so, you know firsthand the blessings that He offers those who worship Him consistently and sincerely. But, if you have unintentionally allowed the hustle and bustle of your busy day to come between you and God, then you must slow down, take a deep breath, and rearrange your priorities.

God loved this world so much that He sent His Son to save it. Now only one real question remains for you: what will you do in response to God's love? The answer should be obvious: God must come first in your life. He is the giver of all good things, and He is the One who sent His Son so that you might have eternal life. He deserves your prayers, your obedience, your stewardship, and your love—and He deserves these things all day every day, not just on Sunday mornings.

If you can't seem to find time for God, then you're simply too busy for your own good. God is never too busy for you, and you should never be too busy for Him.

Marie T. Freeman

Cultivating God's Gifts

I remind you to fan into flame the gift of God.

2 Timothy 1:6 NIV

The gifts that you possess are gifts from the Giver of all things good. Do you have a spiritual gift? Share it. Do you have a testimony about the things that Christ has done for you? Don't leave your story untold. Do you possess financial resources? Share them. Do you have particular talents? Hone your skills and use them for God's glory.

When you hoard the treasures that God has given you, you live in rebellion against His commandments. But, when you obey God by sharing His gifts freely and without fanfare, you invite Him to bless you more and more. Today, be a faithful steward of your talents and treasures. And then prepare yourself for even greater blessings that are sure to come.

It is the definition of joy to be able to offer back to God the essence of what he's placed in you, be that creativity or a love of ideas or a compassionate heart or the gift of hospitality.

Paula Rinehart

God Is at Work

The Lord will work out his plans for my life—for your faithful love, O Lord, endures forever.

Psalm 138:8 NLT

Whether you realize it or not, God is busily working in you and through you. He has things He wants you to do and people He wants you to help. Your assignment, should you choose to accept it, is to seek the will of God and to follow it.

Elisabeth Elliot said, "I believe that in every time and place it is within our power to acquiesce in the will of God—and what peace it brings to do so!" And Corrie ten Boom observed, "Surrendering to the Lord is not a tremendous sacrifice, not an agonizing performance. It is the most sensible thing you can do."

So, as you make plans for the future, make sure that your plans conform to God's plans—that's the safest and best way to live.

I find the doing of the will of God leaves me no time for disputing about His plans.

George MacDonald

He Provides

The Lord is my rock and my fortress and my deliverer; the God of my strength, in whom I will trust.

2 Samuel 22:2-3 NKJV

You know from firsthand experience that life is not always easy. But as a recipient of God's grace, you also know that you are protected by a loving Heavenly Father.

In times of trouble, God will comfort you; in times of sorrow, He will dry your tears. When you are troubled, or weak, or sorrowful, God is neither distant nor disinterested. To the contrary, God is always present and always vitally engaged in the events of your life. Reach out to Him, and build your future on the rock that cannot be shaken . . . trust in God and rely upon His provisions. He can provide everything you really need . . . and far, far more.

God will never let you sink under your circumstances. He always provides a safety net and His love always encircles.

Barbara Johnson

Giving Thanks to the Giver

Is anyone happy? Let him sing songs of praise.

James 5:13 NIV

The 100th Psalm reminds us that the entire earth should "Shout for joy to the Lord." As God's children, we are blessed beyond measure, but sometimes, as busy people living in a demanding world, we are slow to count our gifts and even slower to give thanks to the Giver.

Our blessings include life and health, family and friends, freedom and possessions—for starters. And, the gifts we receive from God are multiplied when we share them. May we always give thanks to God for His blessings, and may we always demonstrate our gratitude by sharing our gifts with others.

The 118th Psalm reminds us that, "This is the day which the LORD has made; let us rejoice and be glad in it" (v. 24, NASB). May we celebrate this day and the One who created it.

Our God is the sovereign Creator of the universe! He loves us as His own children and has provided every good thing we have; He is worthy of our praise every moment.

Shirley Dobson

Quiet Time

In quietness and confidence shall be your strength.

Isaiah 30:15 NKJV

In the first chapter of Mark, we read that in the darkness of the early morning hours, Jesus went to a solitary place and prayed. So, too, should we. But sometimes, finding quiet moments of solitude is difficult indeed.

Has the busy pace of life robbed you of the peace that might otherwise be yours through Jesus Christ? Nothing is more important than the time you spend with your Savior. So be still and claim the inner peace that is your spiritual birthright: the peace of Jesus Christ. It is offered freely; it has been paid for in full; it is yours for the asking. So ask. And then share.

Faithful prayer warriors and devoted Bible lovers will tell you that their passion for disciplined quiet time with the Lord is not a sign of strength but an admission of weakness—a hard-earned realization that they are nothing on their own compared with who they are after they've been with him.

Doris Greig

When Life Is Difficult

Be strong and courageous. Do not be terrified; do not be discouraged, for the LORD your God will be with you wherever you go.

Joshua 1:9 NIV

Life can be difficult and discouraging at times. During our darkest moments, God offers us strength and courage if we turn our hearts and our prayers to Him.

As believing Christians, we have every reason to live courageously. After all, the ultimate battle has already been fought and won on the cross at Calvary. But sometimes, because we are imperfect human beings who possess imperfect faith, we fall prey to fear and doubt. The answer to our fears, of course, is God.

The next time you find your courage tested to the limit, remember that God is as near as your next breath. He is your shield and your strength; He is your protector and your deliverer. Call upon Him in your hour of need and then be comforted. Whatever your challenge, whatever your trouble, God can handle it!

If God has you in the palm of his hand and your real life is secure in him, then you can venture forth—into the places and relationships, the challenges, the very heart of the storm—and you will be safe there.

Paula Rinehart

The Importance of Discipline

For God has not given us a spirit of fear and timidity, but of power, love, and self-discipline. So you must never be ashamed to tell others about our Lord.

2 Timothy 1:7-8 NLT

Wise folks understand the importance of discipline. In Proverbs 28:19, the message is clear: "Those who work their land will have plenty of food, but the ones who chase empty dreams instead will end up poor" (NCV).

If we work diligently and faithfully, we can expect a bountiful harvest. But we must never expect the harvest to precede the labor.

Poet Mary Frances Butts advised, "Build a little fence of trust around today. Fill each space with loving work, and therein stay." And her words still apply.

Thoughtful people understand that God doesn't reward laziness or misbehavior. To the contrary, God expects His children (of all ages) to lead disciplined lives . . . and when they do, He rewards them.

I believe the reason so many are failing today is that they have not disciplined themselves to read God's Word consistently, day in and day out, and to apply it to every situation in life.

Kay Arthur

Celebrating Others

Let us think about each other and help each other to show love and do good deeds.

Hebrews 10:24 NCV

Do you delight in the victories of others? You should. Each day provides countless opportunities to encourage others and to praise their good works. When you do so, you not only spread seeds of joy and happiness, you also obey the commandments of God's Holy Word.

Life is a team sport, and all of us need occasional pats on the back from our teammates. As Christians, we are called upon to spread the Good News of Christ, and we are also called to spread a message of encouragement and hope to the world.

Today, let us be cheerful Christians with smiles on our faces and encouraging words on our lips. By blessing others, we also bless ourselves, and, at the same time, we honor the One who gave His life for us.

True friends will always lift you higher and challenge you to walk in a manner pleasing to our Lord.

Lisa Bevere

Big Dreams

With God's power working in us, God can do much, much more than anything we can ask or imagine.

Ephesians 3:20 NCV

She was born in rural Mississippi and lived with her grandmother in a house that had no indoor plumbing. She made it to college in Nashville, where she got her start in television. Over time, she moved to the top of her profession, and her show, *Oprah*, was an unparalleled hit.

When questioned about her journey to the top, Oprah said, "God can dream a bigger dream than we can dream for ourselves." She was right. So try Oprah's formula: increase the size of your dreams. Because the Good Lord's plan for each of us is big, very big. But it's up to us to accept the part, to step up on stage, and to perform.

The future lies all before us. Shall it only be a slight advance upon what we usually do? Ought it not to be a bound, a leap forward to altitudes of endeavor and success undreamed of before?

Annie Armstrong

Obeying God

And we pray this in order that you may live a life worthy of the Lord and may please him in every way: bearing fruit in every good work, growing in the knowledge of God.

Colossians 1:10 NIV

Life is a series of decisions and choices. Each day, we make countless decisions that can bring us closer to God . . . or not. When we live according to God's commandments, we earn for ourselves the abundance and peace that He intends for our lives. But, when we turn our backs upon God by disobeying Him, we bring needless suffering upon ourselves and our families.

Do you seek God's peace and His blessings? Then obey Him. When you're faced with a difficult choice or a powerful temptation, seek God's counsel and trust the counsel He gives. Invite God into your heart and live according to His commandments. When you do, you will be blessed today, and tomorrow, and forever.

Never use your problem as an excuse for bad attitudes or behavior.

Joyce Meyer

Spiritual Growth

Grow in grace and understanding of our Master and Savior, Jesus Christ. Glory to the Master, now and forever! Yes!

2 Peter 3:18 MSG

If we are to grow as Christians and as individuals, we need both knowledge and wisdom. Knowledge is found in textbooks. Wisdom, on the other hand, is found in God's Word and in the carefully-chosen words of loving family members and friends. Knowledge is an important building block in a well-lived life, and it pays rich dividends both personally and professionally. But, wisdom is even more important because it refashions not only the mind, but also the heart.

When it comes to your faith, God doesn't intend for you to stand still. As a Christian, you should continue to grow in the love and the knowledge of your Savior as long as you live. How? By studying God's Word every day, by obeying His commandments, and by allowing His Son to reign over your heart.

In a special way, human beings . . . being made in the image of God, only become real human beings, are only able to grow and thrive as human beings as they also yearn for God.

Roberta Bondi

Filled with Temptations

Look straight ahead, and fix your eyes on what lies before you. Mark out a straight path for your feet; then stick to the path and stay safe. Don't get sidetracked; keep your feet from following evil.

Proverbs 4:25-27 NLT

If you stop to think about it, the cold, hard evidence is right in front of your eyes: you live in a temptation-filled world. The devil is out on the street, hard at work, causing pain and heartache in more ways than ever before. Here in the 21st century, the bad guys are working around the clock to lead you astray. That's why you must remain vigilant.

In a letter to believers, Peter offered a stern warning: "Your adversary, the devil, prowls around like a roaring lion, seeking someone to devour" (1 Peter 5:8 NASB). What was true then is equally true now. Satan tempts his prey and then devours them. As Christians, we must beware. And, if we seek righteousness in our own lives, we must earnestly wrap ourselves in the protection of God's Holy Word. When we do, we are secure.

We can't stop the Adversary from whispering in our ears, but we can refuse to listen, and we can definitely refuse to respond.

Liz Curtis Higgs

Acceptance Today

I have learned to be content whatever the circumstances.

Philippians 4:11 NIV

Are you embittered by a personal tragedy that you did not deserve and cannot understand? If so, it's time to accept the unchangeable past and to have faith in the promise of tomorrow. It's time to trust God completely—and it's time to reclaim the peace—His peace—that can and should be yours.

On occasion, you will be confronted with situations that you simply don't understand. But God does. And He has a reason for everything that He does.

God doesn't explain Himself in ways that we, as mortals with limited insight and clouded vision, can comprehend. So, instead of understanding every aspect of God's unfolding plan for our lives and our universe, we must be satisfied to trust Him completely. We cannot know God's motivations, nor can we understand His actions. We can, however, trust Him, and we must.

Faith is the willingness to receive whatever he wants to give, or the willingness not to have what he does not want to give.

Elisabeth Elliot

Asking for Wisdom

If you need wisdom—if you want to know what God wants you to do—ask him, and he will gladly tell you. He will not resent your asking.

James 1:5 NLT

How often do you ask God for His help and His wisdom? Occasionally? Intermittently? Whenever you experience a crisis? Hopefully not. Hopefully, you've acquired the habit of asking for God's assistance early and often. And hopefully, you have learned to seek His guidance in every aspect of your life.

The Bible promises that God will guide you if you let Him. Your job is to let Him. But sometimes, you will be tempted to do otherwise. Sometimes, you'll be tempted to go along with the crowd; other times, you'll be tempted to do things your way, not God's way. When you feel those temptations, resist them.

God stands at the door and waits. When you knock, He opens. When you ask, He answers. Your task, of course, is to seek His guidance prayerfully, confidently, and often.

By asking in Jesus' name, we're making a request not only in His authority, but also for His interests and His benefit.

Shirley Dobson

Beyond Blame

Get rid of all bitterness, rage, anger, harsh words, and slander, as well as all types of malicious behavior.

Ephesians 4:31 NLT

To blame others for our own problems is the height of futility. Yet blaming others is a favorite human pastime. Why? Because blaming is much easier than fixing, and criticizing others is so much easier than improving ourselves. So instead of solving our problems legitimately (by doing the work required to solve them) we are inclined to fret, to blame, and to criticize, while doing precious little else. When we do, our problems, quite predictably, remain unsolved.

Have you acquired the bad habit of blaming others for problems that you could or should solve yourself? If so, you are not only disobeying God's Word, you are also wasting your own precious time. So, instead of looking for someone to blame, look for something to fix, and then get busy fixing it. And as you consider your own situation, remember this: God has a way of helping those who help themselves, but He doesn't spend much time helping those who don't.

You'll never win the blame game, so why even bother to play?

Marie T. Freeman

Focusing on God

Give your entire attention to what God is doing right now, and don't get worked up about what may or may not happen tomorrow. God will help you deal with whatever hard things come up when the time comes.

Matthew 6:34 MSG

All of us may find our courage tested by disappointments and tragedies in life. Ours is a world filled with uncertainty, hardship, sickness, and danger. Trouble, it seems, is never too far from the front door.

When we focus upon our fears and our doubts, we may find many reasons to lie awake at night and fret about the uncertainties of the coming day. A better strategy, of course, is to focus not upon our fears, but instead upon our God.

God is as near as your next breath, and He is in control. He offers salvation to all His children, including you. God is your shield and your strength; you are His forever. So don't focus your thoughts upon the fears of the day. Instead, trust God's plan and His eternal love for you. And remember: God is good, and He has the last word.

His hand on me is a father's hand, gently guiding and encouraging. His hand lets me know he is with me, so I am not afraid.

Mary Morrison Suggs

The Wisdom of Moderation

Moderation is better than muscle, self-control better than political power.

Proverbs 16:32 MSG

Moderation and wisdom are traveling companions. If we are wise, we must learn to temper our appetites, our desires, and our impulses. When we do, we are blessed, in part, because God has created a world in which temperance is rewarded and intemperance is inevitably punished.

Would you like to improve your life? Then harness your appetites and restrain your impulses. Moderation is difficult, of course; it is especially difficult in a prosperous society such as ours. But the rewards of moderation are numerous and long-lasting. Claim those rewards today.

No one can force you to moderate your appetites. The decision to live temperately (and wisely) is yours and yours alone. And so are the consequences.

Contentment has a way of quieting insatiable desires.

Mary Hunt

You Must Persevere Like Him

If you do nothing in a difficult time, your strength is limited.

Proverbs 24:10 HCSB

In a world filled with roadblocks and stumbling blocks, we need strength, courage, and perseverance. And, as an example of perfect perseverance, we need look no further than our Savior, Jesus Christ.

Jesus finished what He began. Despite the torture He endured, despite the shame of the cross, Jesus was steadfast in His faithfulness to God. We, too, must remain faithful, especially during times of hardship.

Perhaps you are in a hurry for God to reveal His plans for your life. If so, be forewarned: God operates on His own timetable, not yours. Sometimes, God may answer your prayers with silence, and when He does, you must patiently persevere. In times of trouble, you must remain steadfast and trust in the merciful goodness of your Heavenly Father. Whatever your problem, He can handle it. Your job is to keep persevering until He does.

By perseverance the snail reached the ark.

C. H. Spurgeon

Pause and Praise

And those who have reason to be thankful should continually sing praises to the Lord.

James 5:13 NLT

Because we have been saved by God's only Son, we must never lose hope in the priceless gifts of eternal love and eternal life. And, because we are so richly blessed, we must approach our Heavenly Father with reverence and thanksgiving.

Sometimes, in our rush "to get things done," we simply don't stop long enough to pause and thank our Creator for the countless blessings He has bestowed upon us. But when we slow down and express our gratitude to the One who made us, we enrich our own lives and the lives of those around us.

Thanksgiving should become a habit, a regular part of our daily routines. God has blessed us beyond measure, and we owe Him everything, including our eternal praise. Let us praise Him today, tomorrow, and throughout eternity.

How delightful a teacher, but gentle a provider, how bountiful a giver is my Father! Praise, praise to Thee, O manifested Most High.

Jim Elliot

Working for the Harvest

So I saw that the best thing people can do is to enjoy their work, because that is all they have. No one can help another person see what will happen in the future.

Ecclesiastes 3:22 NCV

Once the season for planting is upon us, the time to plant seeds is when we make time to plant seeds. And when it comes to planting God's seeds in the soil of eternity, the only certain time that we have is now. Yet because we are fallible human beings with limited vision and misplaced priorities, we may be tempted to delay.

If we hope to reap a bountiful harvest for God, for our families, and for ourselves, we must plant now by defeating a dreaded human frailty: the habit of procrastination. Procrastination often results from our shortsighted attempts to postpone temporary discomfort.

A far better strategy is this: Whatever "it" is, do it now. When you do, you won't have to worry about "it" later.

Never fail to do something because you don't feel like it. Sometimes you just have to do it now, and you'll feel like it later.

Marie T. Freeman

Real Repentance

Come back to the LORD and live!

Amos 5:6 NLT

Genuine repentance requires more than simply offering God apologies for our misdeeds. Real repentance may start with feelings of sorrow and remorse, but it ends only when we turn away from the sin that has heretofore distanced us from our Creator. In truth, we offer our most meaningful apologies to God, not with our words, but with our actions. As long as we are still engaged in sin, we may be "repenting," but we have not fully "repented."

Is there an aspect of your life that is distancing you from your God? If so, ask for His forgiveness, and—just as importantly—stop sinning. Then, wrap yourself in the protection of God's Word. When you do, you will be secure.

Repentance involves a radical change of heart and mind in which we agree with God's evaluation of our sin and then take specific action to align ourselves with His will.

Henry Blackaby

Heeding His Call

I, therefore, the prisoner in the Lord, urge you to walk worthy of the calling you have received.

Ephesians 4:1 HCSB

It is terribly important that you heed God's calling by discovering and developing your talents and your spiritual gifts. If you seek to make a difference—and if you seek to bear eternal fruit—you must discover your gifts and begin using them for the glory of God.

Every believer has at least one gift. In John 15:16, Jesus says, "You did not choose Me, but I chose you and appointed you that you should go and bear fruit, and that your fruit should remain, that whatever you ask the Father in My name He may give you." Have you found your special calling? If not, keep searching and keep praying until you find it. God has important work for you to do, and the time to begin that work is now.

God never calls without enabling us. In other words, if he calls you to do something, he makes it possible for you to do it.

Luci Swindoll

Your Response to His Love

This is how much God loved the world: He gave his Son, his one and only Son. And this is why: so that no one need be destroyed; by believing in him anyone can have a whole and lasting life.

John 3:16 MSG

God's love for you is deeper and more profound than you can fathom. And now, precisely because you are a wondrous creation treasured by God, a question presents itself: What will you do in response to God's love? Will you ignore it or embrace it? Will you return it or neglect it? The decision, of course, is yours and yours alone.

When you embrace God's love, you are forever changed. When you embrace God's love, you feel differently about yourself, your neighbors, and your world. When you embrace God's love, you share His message and you obey His commandments.

When you accept the Father's grace and share His love, you are blessed here on earth and throughout all eternity. Accept His love today.

To be loved by God is the highest relationship, the highest achievement, and the highest position of life.

Henry Blackaby and Claude King

His Perspective and Yours

Since you have been raised to new life with Christ, set your sights on the realities of heaven, where Christ sits at God's right hand in the place of honor and power.

Colossians 3:1 NLT

If a temporary loss of perspective has left you worried, exhausted, or both, it's time to readjust your thought patterns. Negative thoughts are habit-forming; thankfully, so are positive ones. With practice, you can form the habit of focusing on God's priorities and your own possibilities. When you do, you'll soon discover that you will spend less time fretting about your challenges and more time praising God for His gifts.

When you call upon the Lord and prayerfully seek His will, He will give you wisdom and perspective. When you make God's priorities your priorities, He will direct your steps and calm your fears. So today and every day hereafter, pray for a sense of balance and perspective. And remember: no problems are too big for God—and that includes yours.

Don't quit. For if you do, you may miss the answer to your prayers.

Max Lucado

Pray Always

Watch therefore, and pray always that you may be counted worthy . . . .

Luke 21:36 NKJV

Jesus made it clear to His disciples: they should pray always. And so should we. Genuine, heartfelt prayer changes things and it changes us. When we lift our hearts to our Father in heaven, we open ourselves to a never-ending source of divine wisdom and infinite love.

Do you have questions that you simply can't answer? Ask for the guidance of your Father in heaven. Do you sincerely seek the gift of everlasting love and eternal life? Accept the grace of God's only begotten Son. Whatever your need, no matter how great or small, pray about it. Instead of waiting for mealtimes or bedtimes, follow the instruction of your Savior: pray always and never lose heart. And remember: God is not just near; He is here, and He's ready to talk with you. Now!

He who kneels most stands best.

D. L. Moody

Living on Purpose

It is God who works in you to will and to act according to his good purpose.

Philippians 2:13 NIV

Life is best lived on purpose. And purpose, like everything else in the universe, begins with God. Whether you realize it or not, God has a plan for your life, a divine calling, a direction in which He is leading you. When you welcome God into your heart and establish a genuine relationship with Him, He will begin, in time, to make His purposes known.

Sometimes, God's intentions will be clear to you; other times, God's plan will seem uncertain at best. But even on those difficult days when you are unsure which way to turn, you must never lose sight of these overriding facts: God created you for a reason; He has important work for you to do; and He's waiting patiently for you to do it.

And the next step is up to you.

There is a path before you that you alone can walk. There is a purpose that you alone can fulfill.

Karla Dornacher

Rest and Recharge

Come unto me, all ye that labor and are heavy laden, and I will give you rest.

Matthew 11:28 KJV

Even the most inspired Christians can, from time to time, find themselves running on empty. The demands of daily life can drain us of our strength and rob us of the joy that is rightfully ours in Christ. When we find ourselves tired, discouraged, or worse, there is a source from which we can draw the power needed to recharge our spiritual batteries. That source is God.

God expects us to work hard, but He also intends for us to rest. When we fail to take the rest that we need, we do a disservice to ourselves and to our families.

Is your spiritual battery running low? Is your energy on the wane? Are your emotions frayed? If so, it's time to turn your thoughts and your prayers to God. And when you're finished, it's time to rest.

Prescription for a happier and healthier life: resolve to slow down your pace; learn to say no gracefully; resist the temptation to chase after more pleasure, more hobbies, and more social entanglements.

James Dobson

The Source of Strength

Have you not known? Have you not heard? The everlasting God, the Lord, the Creator of the ends of the earth, neither faints nor is weary. His understanding is unsearchable. He gives power to the weak, and to those who have no might He increases strength.

Isaiah 40:28-29 NKJV

God is a never-ending source of strength and courage if we call upon Him. When we are weary, He gives us strength. When we see no hope, God reminds us of His promises. When we grieve, God wipes away our tears.

Do you feel overwhelmed by today's responsibilities? Do you feel pressured by the ever-increasing demands of 21st-century life? Then turn your concerns and your prayers over to God. He knows your needs, and He has promised to meet those needs. Whatever your circumstances, God will protect you and care for you . . . if you let Him. Invite Him into your heart and allow Him to renew your spirits. When you trust Him and Him alone, He will never fail you.

God gives us always strength enough, and sense enough, for everything he wants us to do.

John Ruskin

The Gift of Time

Hard work means prosperity; only fools idle away their time.

Proverbs 12:11 NLT

Time is a nonrenewable gift from God. But sometimes, we treat our time here on earth as if it were not a gift at all: We may be tempted to invest our lives in trivial pursuits and petty diversions. But our Father beckons each of us to a higher calling.

An important element of our stewardship to God is the way that we choose to spend the time He has entrusted to us. Each waking moment holds the potential to do a good deed, to say a kind word, or to offer a heartfelt prayer. Our challenge, as believers, is to use our time wisely in the service of God's work and in accordance with His plan for our lives.

Each day is a special treasure to be savored and celebrated. May we—as Christians who have so much to celebrate—never fail to praise our Creator by rejoicing in His glorious creation and by using it wisely.

Overcommitment and time pressures are the greatest destroyers of marriages and families. It takes time to develop any friendship, whether with a loved one or with God himself.

James Dobson

When It's Hard to Be Happy

Be cheerful. Keep things in good repair. Keep your spirits up. Think in harmony. Be agreeable. Do all that, and the God of love and peace will be with you for sure.

2 Corinthians 13:11 MSG

On some days, it's hard to be happy or cheerful. Sometimes, as the demands of the world increase and our energy sags, we feel less like "cheering up" and more like "tearing up." But even in our darkest hours, we can turn to God, and He will give us comfort.

Few things in life are more sad, or, for that matter, more absurd, than a grumpy Christian. Jesus promises us lives of abundance and joy, but He does not force His joy upon us. We must claim His joy for ourselves, and when we do, Jesus, in turn, fills our spirits with His power and His love.

When we earnestly commit ourselves to the Savior of mankind, when we place Jesus at the center of our lives and trust Him as our personal Savior, He will transform us, not just for today, but for all eternity. Then we, as God's children, can share Christ's joy and His message with a world that needs both.

It is not fitting, when one is in God's service, to have a gloomy face or a chilling look.

St. Francis of Assisi

Living Courageously

So do not fear, for I am with you; do not be dismayed, for I am your God. I will strengthen you and help you; I will uphold you with my righteous right hand.

Isaiah 41:10 NIV

Christians have every reason to live courageously. After all, the final battle has already been won on the cross at Calvary. But even dedicated followers of Christ may find their courage tested by the inevitable disappointments and fears that visit the lives of believers and non-believers alike.

When you find yourself worried about the challenges of today or the uncertainties of tomorrow, you must ask yourself whether or not you are ready to place your concerns and your life in God's all-powerful, all-knowing, all-loving hands. If the answer to that question is yes—as it should be—then you can draw courage today from the source of strength that never fails: your Heavenly Father.

With each new experience of letting God be in control, we gain courage and reinforcement for daring to do it again and again.

Gloria Gaither

Difficult Decisions

Now if any of you lacks wisdom, he should ask God, who gives to all generously and without criticizing, and it will be given to him.

James 1:5 HCSB

Are you facing a difficult decision, a troubling circumstance, or a powerful temptation? If so, it's time to step back, to stop focusing on the world, and to focus, instead, on the will of your Father in heaven. The world will often lead you astray, but God will not. His counsel leads you to Himself, which, of course, is the path He has always intended for you to take.

Everyday living is an exercise in decision-making. Today and every day you must make choices: choices about what you will do, what you will worship, and how you will think. When in doubt, make choices that you sincerely believe will bring you to a closer relationship with God. And if you're uncertain of your next step, pray about it. When you do, answers will come. And you may rest assured that when God answers prayer, His answers are the right ones for you.

The principle of making no decision without prayer keeps me from rushing in and committing myself before I consult God.

Elizabeth George

The Need to Persevere

Patient endurance is what you need now, so you will continue to do God's will. Then you will receive all that he has promised.

Hebrews 10:36 NLT

If you've led a perfect life with absolutely no foul ups, blunders, mistakes, or flops, you can skip this chapter. But if you're like the rest of us, you know that occasional disappointments and failures are an inevitable part of life. These setbacks are simply the price of growing up and learning about life. But even when you experience bitter disappointments, you must never lose faith.

When we encounter the inevitable difficulties of life, God stands ready to protect us. And, while we are waiting for God's plans to unfold, we can be comforted in the knowledge that our Creator can overcome any obstacle, even if we cannot.

I learned as never before that persistent calling upon the Lord breaks through every stronghold of the devil, for nothing is impossible with God. For Christians in these troubled times, there is simply no other way.

Jim Cymbala

Praising the Savior

At the name of Jesus every knee should bow, of those in heaven, and of those on earth, and of those under the earth, and that every tongue should confess that Jesus Christ is Lord, to the glory of God the Father.

Philippians 2:10-11 NKJV

The words by Fanny Crosby are familiar: "This is my story, this is my song, praising my Savior, all the day long." As believers who have been saved by the blood of a risen Christ, we must do exactly as the song instructs: We must praise our Savior time and time again throughout the day. Worship and praise should be a part of everything we do. Otherwise, we quickly lose perspective as we fall prey to the demands of everyday life.

Do you sincerely desire to be a worthy servant of the One who has given you eternal love and eternal life? Then praise Him for who He is and for what He has done for you. And don't just praise Him on Sunday morning. Praise Him all day long, every day, for as long as you live . . . and then for all eternity.

The time for universal praise is sure to come some day. Let us begin to do our part now.

Hannah Whitall Smith

Spiritual Abundance

These things have I spoken unto you, that my joy might remain in you, and that your joy might be full.

John 15:11 KJV

God does not promise us abundance. He promises that we "might have life" and that we "might have it more abundantly" if we accept His grace, His blessings, and His Son (John 10:10). When we commit our hearts and our days to the One who created us, we experience spiritual abundance through the grace and sacrifice of His Son, Jesus. But, when we focus our thoughts and energies, not upon God's perfect will for our lives, but instead upon our own unending assortments of earthly needs and desires, we inevitably forfeit the spiritual abundance that might otherwise be ours.

Today and every day, seek God's will for your life and follow it. Today, turn your worries and your concerns over to your Heavenly Father. Today, seek God's wisdom, follow His commandments, trust His judgment, and honor His Son. When you do, spiritual abundance will be yours, not just for this day, but for all eternity.

God loves you and wants you to experience peace and life—abundant and eternal.

Billy Graham

Bearing Witness to the Truth

But the natural man does not welcome what comes from God's Spirit, because it is foolishness to him; he is not able to know it since it is evaluated spiritually. The spiritual person, however, can evaluate everything, yet he himself cannot be evaluated by anyone.

1 Corinthians 2:14-15 HCSB

When God's spirit touches our hearts, we are confronted by a powerful force: the awesome, irresistible force of God's Truth. In response to that force, we will either follow God's lead by allowing Him to guide our thoughts and deeds, or we will resist God's calling and accept the consequences of our rebellion.

Today, as you fulfill the responsibilities that God has placed before you, ask yourself this question: "Do my thoughts and actions bear witness to the ultimate Truth that God has placed in my heart, or am I allowing the pressures of everyday life to overwhelm me?" It's a profound question that only you can answer. You be the judge.

We have in Jesus Christ a perfect example of how to put God's truth into practice.

Bill Bright

Beyond Mediocrity

Therefore by their fruits you will know them.

Matthew 7:20 NKJV

God's Word teaches us the value of hard work. In his second letter to the Thessalonians, Paul warns, "if any would not work, neither should he eat" (3:10 KJV). And the Book of Proverbs proclaims, "One who is slack in his work is brother to one who destroys" (18:9 NIV). In short, God has created a world in which diligence is rewarded but sloth is not. So, whatever it is that you choose to do, do it with commitment, excitement, and vigor.

Hard work is not simply a proven way to get ahead, it's also part of God's plan for you. God did not create you for a life of mediocrity; He created you for far greater things. Reaching for greater things usually requires work and lots of it, which is perfectly fine with God. After all, He knows that you're up to the task, and He has big plans for you if you possess a loving heart and willing hands.

I am more and more persuaded that all that is required of us is faithful seed-sowing. The harvest is bound to follow.

Annie Armstrong

He Does Not Change

One Lord, one faith, one baptism, one God and Father of all, who is above all and through all and in all.

Ephesians 4:5-6 HCSB

We live in a world that is always changing, but we worship a God that never changes—thank goodness! As believers, we can be comforted in the knowledge that our Heavenly Father is the rock that simply cannot be moved: "I am the Lord, I do not change" (Malachi 3:6 NKJV).

Are you facing difficult circumstances or unwelcome changes? If so, please remember that God is far bigger than any problem you may face. So, instead of worrying about life's inevitable challenges, put your faith in the Father and His only begotten Son: "Jesus Christ is the same yesterday, today, and forever" (Hebrews 13:8 HCSB). And rest assured: It is precisely because your Savior does not change that you can face your challenges with courage for this day and hope for the future.

Let nothing disturb you, nothing frighten you; all things are passing; God never changes.

St. Teresa of Avila

Optimistic Christianity

Make me to hear joy and gladness.

Psalm 51:8 KJV

Are you an optimistic, hopeful, enthusiastic Christian? You should be. After all, as a believer, you have every reason to be optimistic about life here on earth and life eternal. As C. H. Spurgeon observed, "Our hope in Christ for the future is the mainstream of our joy." But sometimes, you may find yourself pulled down by the inevitable demands and worries of life. If you find yourself discouraged, exhausted, or both, then it's time to take your concerns to God. When you do, He will lift your spirits and renew your strength.

Today, make this promise to yourself and keep it: vow to be a hope-filled Christian. Think optimistically about your life, your profession, your family, and your future. Trust your hopes, not your fears. Take time to celebrate God's glorious creation. And then, when you've filled your heart with hope and gladness, share your optimism with others. They'll be better for it, and so will you.

There is wisdom in the habit of looking at the bright side of life.

Father Flanagan

The Power of Habits

Do not be deceived: "Evil company corrupts good habits."

1 Corinthians 15:33 NKJV

It's an old saying and a true one: First, you make your habits, and then your habits make you. Some habits will inevitably bring you closer to God; other habits will lead you away from the path He has chosen for you. If you sincerely desire to improve your spiritual health, you must honestly examine the habits that make up the fabric of your day. And you must abandon those habits that are displeasing to God.

If you trust God, and if you keep asking for His help, He can transform your life. If you sincerely ask Him to help you, the same God who created the universe will help you defeat the harmful habits that have heretofore defeated you. So, if at first you don't succeed, keep praying. God is listening, and He's ready to help you become a better person if you ask Him . . . so ask today.

Prayer is a habit. Worship is a habit. Kindness is a habit. And if you want to please God, you'd better make sure that these habits are your habits.

Marie T. Freeman

Swamped by Possessions

Don't be obsessed with getting more material things. Be relaxed with what you have.

Hebrews 13:5 MSG

Do you sometimes feel swamped by your possessions? Do you seem to be spending more and more time keeping track of the things you own while making mental notes of the things you intend to buy? If so, here's a word of warning: your fondness for material possessions is getting in the way of your relationships—your relationships with the people around you and your relationship with God.

Society teaches us to honor possessions . . . God teaches us to honor people. And if we seek to be worthy followers of Christ, we must never invest too much energy in the acquisition of "stuff." Earthly riches are here today and all too soon gone. Our real riches, of course, are in heaven, and that's where we should focus our thoughts and our energy.

A society that pursues pleasure runs the risk of raising expectations ever higher, so that true contentment always lies tantalizingly out of reach.

Philip Yancey and Paul Brand

He Wants Your Attention

Give your entire attention to what God is doing right now, and don't get worked up about what may or may not happen tomorrow. God will help you deal with whatever hard things come up when the time comes.

Matthew 6:34 MSG

Is yours a life of moderation or accumulation? Are you more interested in the possessions you can acquire or in the person you can become? The answers to these questions will determine the direction of your day and, in time, the direction of your life.

Ours is a highly complicated society, a place where people and corporations vie for your attention, for your time, and for your dollars. Don't let them succeed in complicating your life! Keep your eyes focused instead upon God.

If your material possessions are somehow distancing you from God, discard them. If your outside interests leave you too little time for your family or your Creator, slow down the merry-go-round, or better yet, get off the merry-go-round completely. Remember: God wants your full attention, and He wants it today, so don't let anybody or anything get in His way.

Whatever we focus on determines what we become.

E. Stanley Jones

Using Your Talents

God has given gifts to each of you from his great variety of spiritual gifts. Manage them well so that God's generosity can flow through you.

1 Peter 4:10 NLT

Your talents, resources, and opportunities are all gifts from the Giver of all things good. And the best way to say "Thank You" for these gifts is to use them.

Do you have a particular talent? Hone your skill and use it. Do you possess financial resources? Share them. Have you been blessed by a particular opportunity, or have you experienced unusual good fortune? Use your good fortune to help others.

When you share the gifts God has given you—and when you share them freely and without fanfare—you invite God to bless you more and more. So today, do yourself and the world a favor: be a faithful steward of your talents and treasures. And then prepare yourself for even greater blessings that are sure to come.

You are the only person on earth who can use your ability.

Zig Ziglar

Be Transformed

And do not be conformed to this world, but be transformed by the renewing of your mind, that you may prove what is that good and acceptable and perfect will of God.

Romans 12:2 NKJV

Believers who fashion their days around Jesus are transformed: They see the world differently; they act differently; and they feel differently about themselves and their neighbors.

Thoughtful believers face the inevitable challenges and disappointments of each day armed with the joy of Christ and the promise of salvation. So whatever this day holds for you, begin it and end it with God as your partner and Christ as your Savior. And throughout the day, give thanks to the One who created you and saved you. God's love for you is infinite. Accept it joyously and be thankful.

If God can fashion the mountains, if God can keep the sun in its orbit, if God can split a sea and dry the ground beneath it so an entire nation can cross, do you doubt that he can transform your character?

Bill Hybels

Seeking His Wisdom

Wisdom is the principal thing; therefore get wisdom. And in all your getting, get understanding.

Proverbs 4:7 NKJV

Do you seek the wisdom that only God can give? If so, ask Him for it! If you ask God for guidance, He will not withhold it. If you petition Him sincerely, and if you genuinely seek to form a relationship with Him, your Heavenly Father will guide your steps and enlighten your heart. But be forewarned: You will not acquire God's wisdom without obeying His commandments. Why? Because God's wisdom is more than just a collection of thoughts; it is, first and foremost, a way of life.

Wisdom is as wisdom does. So if you sincerely seek God's wisdom, don't be satisfied to learn something; make up your mind to become something. And then, as you allow God to remake you in the image of His Son, you will most surely become wise.

Our first step toward gaining God's wisdom is to know what we do not know; that is, to be aware of our shortcomings.

Dianna Booher

Making Peace with the Past

Do not remember the past events, pay no attention to things of old. Look, I am about to do something new; even now it is coming. Do you not see it? Indeed, I will make a way in the wilderness, rivers in the desert.

Isaiah 43:18-19 HCSB

Have you made peace with your past? If so, congratulations. But, if you are mired in the quicksand of regret, it's time to plan your escape. How can you do so? By accepting what has been and by trusting God for what will be.

Because you are human, you may be slow to forget yesterday's disappointments; if so you are not alone. But if you sincerely seek to focus your hopes and energies on the future, then you must find ways to accept the past, no matter how difficult it may be to do so.

If you have not yet made peace with the past, today is the day to declare an end to all hostilities. When you do, you can then turn your thoughts to the wondrous promises of God and to the glorious future that He has in store for you.

Don't let yesterday use up too much of today.

Dennis Swanberg

What Kind of Example?

You are the light that gives light to the world. . . . In the same way, you should be a light for other people. Live so that they will see the good things you do and will praise your Father in heaven.

Matthew 5:14, 16 NCV

Whether we like it or not, all of us are examples. The question is not whether we will be examples to our families and friends; the question is simply what kind of examples will we be.

What kind of example are you? Are you the kind of person whose life serves as a powerful example of righteousness? Are you a person whose behavior serves as a positive role model for young people? Are you the kind of person whose actions, day in and day out, are based upon integrity, fidelity, and a love for the Lord? If so, you are not only blessed by God, you are also a powerful force for good in a world that desperately needs positive influences such as yours.

Nothing speaks louder or more powerfully than a life of integrity.

Charles Swindoll

His Promises to You

This is my comfort in my affliction: Your promise has given me life.

Psalm 119:50 HCSB

God's promises are found in a book like no other: the Holy Bible. The Bible is a roadmap for life here on earth and for life eternal. As Christians, we are called upon to trust its promises, to follow its commandments, and to share its Good News.

As believers, we must study the Bible daily and meditate upon its meaning for our lives. Otherwise, we deprive ourselves of a priceless gift from our Creator. God's Holy Word is, indeed, a transforming, life-changing, one-of-a-kind treasure. And, a passing acquaintance with the Good Book is insufficient for Christians who seek to obey God's Word and to understand His will.

God has made promises to mankind and to you. God's promises never fail and they never grow old. You must trust those promises and share them with your family, with your friends, and with the world.

The meaning of hope isn't just some flimsy wishing. It's a firm confidence in God's promises—that he will ultimately set things right.

Sheila Walsh

Trusting His Timing

Therefore humble yourselves under the mighty hand of God, that He may exalt you in due time.

1 Peter 5:6 NKJV

If you sincerely wish to be a person of faith, then you must learn to trust God's timing. You will be sorely tempted, however, to do otherwise. Because you are a fallible human being, you are impatient for things to happen. But, God knows better.

God has created a world that unfolds according to His own timetable, not ours . . . thank goodness! We mortals might make a terrible mess of things. God does not.

God's plan does not always happen in the way that we would like or at the time of our own choosing. Our task—as believing Christians who trust in a benevolent, all-knowing Father—is to wait patiently for God to reveal Himself. And reveal Himself He will. Always. But until God's perfect plan is made known, we must walk in faith and never lose hope. And we must continue to trust Him. Always.

God has a designated time when his promise will be fulfilled and the prayer will be answered.

Jim Cymbala

The Self-fulfilling Prophecy

But as for me, I will hope continually, and will praise You yet more and more.

Psalm 71:14 NASB

The self-fulfilling prophecy is alive, well, and living at your house. If you trust God and have faith for the future, your optimistic beliefs will give you direction and motivation. That's one reason that you should never lose hope, but certainly not the only reason. The primary reason that you, as a believer, should never lose hope, is because of God's unfailing promises.

Your thoughts have the power to lift you up or to hold you down. When you acquire the habit of hopeful thinking, you will have acquired a powerful tool for improving your life. So if you find yourself falling into the spiritual traps of worry and discouragement, seek the healing touch of Jesus and the encouraging words of fellow Christians. And if you fall into the terrible habit of negative thinking, think again. After all, God's Word teaches us that Christ can overcome every difficulty (John 16:33). And when God makes a promise, He keeps it.

Great hopes make great men.

Thomas Fuller

You Are Protected

But seek first his kingdom and his righteousness, and all these things will be given to you as well. Therefore do not worry about tomorrow, for tomorrow will worry about itself. Each day has enough trouble of its own.

Matthew 6:33-34 NIV

Because we are fallible human beings, we worry. Even though we, as Christians, have the assurance of salvation—even though we, as Christians, have the promise of God's love and protection—we find ourselves fretting over the countless details of everyday life.

If you are like most folks, you may, on occasion, find yourself worrying about health, about finances, about safety, about relationships, about family, and about countless other challenges of life, some great and some small. Where is the best place to take your worries? Take them to God. Take your troubles to Him, and your fears, and your sorrows. And remember: God is trustworthy . . . and you are protected.

Today is the tomorrow we worried about yesterday.

Dennis Swanberg

Kindness Now

God has chosen you and made you his holy people. He loves you. So always do these things: Show mercy to others, be kind, humble, gentle, and patient.

Colossians 3:12 NCV

Christ showed His love for us by willingly sacrificing His own life so that we might have eternal life: "But God demonstrates his own love for us in this: While we were still sinners, Christ died for us" (Romans 5:8 NIV). We, as Christ's followers, are challenged to share His love with kind words on our lips and praise in our hearts.

Just as Christ has been—and will always be—the ultimate friend to His flock, so should we be Christ-like in the kindness and generosity that we show toward others, especially those who are most in need.

When we walk each day with Jesus—and obey the commandments found in God's Holy Word—we become worthy ambassadors for Christ. When we share the love of Christ, we share a priceless gift with the world. As His servants, we must do no less.

One of the greatest things a man can do for his heavenly Father is to be kind to some of his other children.

Henry Drummond

Do You Believe in Miracles?

With God's power working in us, God can do much, much more than anything we can ask or imagine.

Ephesians 3:20 NCV

Do you believe in an all-powerful God who can do miraculous things in you and through you? You should. But perhaps, as you have faced the inevitable struggles of life you have—without realizing it—placed limitations on God. To do so is a profound mistake. God's power has no such limitations, and He can work mighty miracles in your own life if you let Him.

Do you lack a firm faith in God's power to perform miracles for you and your loved ones? If so, you are attempting to place limitations on a God who has none. Instead of doubting your Heavenly Father, you must place yourself in His hands. Instead of doubting God's power, you must trust it. Expect Him to work miracles, and be watchful. With God, absolutely nothing is impossible, including an amazing assortment of miracles that He stands ready, willing, and perfectly able to perform for you and yours.

To be a Christian is to believe in the impossible. Jesus was God. Jesus was human.

Madeleine L'Engle

Beyond the Frustrations

But now you must also put away all the following: anger, wrath, malice, slander, and filthy language from your mouth.

Colossians 3:8 HCSB

The frustrations of everyday living can sometimes get the better of us, and we allow minor disappointments to cause us major problems. When we allow ourselves to become overly irritated by the inevitable ups and downs of life, we become overstressed, overheated, overanxious, and just plain angry.

As singer Tina Turner once observed, "If you want to be successful, you don't have time for bitterness." And the same can be said for anger.

As the old saying goes, "Anger usually improves nothing but the arch of a cat's back." So don't allow feelings of anger or frustration to rule your life, or, for that matter, your day—your life is simply too short for that, and you deserve much better treatment than that . . . from yourself.

Anger breeds remorse in the heart, discord in the home, bitterness in the community, and confusion in the state.

Billy Graham

A Book Unlike Any Other

Your word is a lamp for my feet and a light on my path.

Psalm 119:105 HCSB

God's Word is unlike any other book. The words of Matthew 4:4 remind us that, "Man shall not live by bread alone but by every word that proceedeth out of the mouth of God" (KJV). As believers, we are instructed to study the Bible and meditate upon its meaning for our lives, yet far too many Bibles are laid aside by well-intentioned believers who would like to study the Bible if they could "just find the time."

Warren Wiersbe observed, "When the child of God looks into the Word of God, he sees the Son of God. And, he is transformed by the Spirit of God to share in the glory of God." God's Holy Word is, indeed, a transforming, life-changing, one-of-a-kind treasure. And it's up to you—and only you—to use it that way.

Study the Bible and observe how the persons behaved and how God dealt with them. There is explicit teaching on every condition of life.

Corrie ten Boom

What's Really Important

Anyone trusting in his riches will fall, but the righteous will flourish like foliage.

Proverbs 11:28 HCSB

In the demanding world in which we live, financial prosperity can be a good thing, but spiritual prosperity is profoundly more important. Yet our society leads us to believe otherwise. The world glorifies material possessions, personal fame, and physical beauty above all else; these things, of course, are totally unimportant to God. God sees the human heart, and that's what is important to Him.

As you establish your priorities for the coming day, remember this: The world will do everything it can to convince you that "things" are important. The world will tempt you to value fortune above faith and possessions above peace. God, on the other hand, will try to convince you that your relationship with Him is all-important. Trust God.

We are made spiritually lethargic by a steady diet of materialism.

Mary Morrison Suggs

Wait for Him

The Lord is wonderfully good to those who wait for him and seek him. So it is good to wait quietly for salvation from the Lord.

Lamentations 3:25-26 NLT

Are you a person in a hurry? If so, you may be in for a few disappointments. Why? Because life has a way of unfolding according to its own timetable, not yours. That's why life requires patience . . . and lots of it!

Lamentations 3:25 reminds us that, "The Lord is wonderfully good to those who wait for him and seek him" (NIV). For most of us, waiting quietly is difficult because we're in such a hurry for things to happen!

The next time you find your patience tested to the limit, slow down, take a deep breath, and relax. Sometimes life can't be hurried—and during those times, patience is indeed a priceless virtue.

Grass that is here today and gone tomorrow does not require much time to mature. A big oak tree that lasts for generations requires much more time to grow and mature. God is concerned about your life through eternity. Allow Him to take all the time He needs to shape you for His purposes. Larger assignments will require longer periods of preparation.

Henry Blackaby

Taking Up His Cross

If anyone would come after me, he must deny himself and take up his cross and follow me.

Mark 8:34 NIV

When Jesus addressed His disciples, He warned that each one must, "take up his cross and follow me." The disciples must have known exactly what the Master meant. In Jesus' day, prisoners were forced to carry their own crosses to the location where they would be put to death. Thus, Christ's message was clear: in order to follow Him, Christ's disciples must deny themselves and, instead, trust Him completely. Nothing has changed since then.

If we are to be dutiful disciples of the One from Galilee, we must trust Him and we must follow Him. Jesus never comes "next." He is always first. He shows us the path of life.

Do you seek to be a worthy disciple of Jesus? Then pick up His cross today and follow in His footsteps. When you do, you can walk with confidence: He will never lead you astray.

God often keeps us on the path by guiding us through the counsel of friends and trusted spiritual advisors.

Bill Hybels

His Peace

But now in Christ Jesus you who once were far off have been brought near by the blood of Christ. For He Himself is our peace.

Ephesians 2:13-14 NKJV

On many occasions, our outer struggles are simply manifestations of the inner conflicts that we feel when we stray from God's path. What's needed is a refresher course in God's promise of peace. The beautiful words of John 14:27 remind us that Jesus offers peace, not as the world gives, but as He alone gives: "Peace I leave with you. My peace I give to you. I do not give to you as the world gives. Your heart must not be troubled or fearful" (HCSB).

As believers, our challenge is straightforward: we should welcome Christ's peace into our hearts and then, as best we can, share His peace with our neighbors.

Today, as a gift to yourself, to your family, and to your friends, invite Christ to preside over every aspect of your life. It's the best way to live and the surest path to peace . . . today and forever.

There is never any peace for those who resist God.

François Fènelon

Asking for His Guidance

Continue to ask, and God will give to you. Continue to search, and you will find. Continue to knock, and the door will open for you.

Matthew 7:7 ICB

Have you fervently asked God for His guidance in every aspect of your life? If so, then you're continually inviting your Creator to reveal Himself in a variety of ways. As a follower of Christ, you must do no less.

Jesus made it clear to His disciples: They should pray always. So should we. Genuine, heartfelt prayer produces powerful changes in us and in our world. When we lift our hearts to our Father in heaven, we open ourselves to a never-ending source of divine wisdom and infinite love.

Do you have questions about your future that you simply can't answer? Ask for the guidance of your Heavenly Father. Do you sincerely seek to know God's purpose for your life? Then ask Him for direction—and keep asking Him every day that you live. Whatever your need, no matter how great or small, pray about it and never lose hope. God is not just near; He is here, and He's ready to talk with you. Now!

Prayer accomplishes more than anything else.

Bill Bright

Getting Past the Regrets

And don't be wishing you were someplace else or with someone else. Where you are right now is God's place for you. Live and obey and love and believe right there.

1 Corinthians 7:17 MSG

Bitterness can destroy you if you let it . . . so don't let it!

If you are caught up in intense feelings of anger or regret, you know all too well the destructive power of these emotions. How can you rid yourself of these feelings? First, you must prayerfully ask God to free you from these feelings. Then, you must learn to catch yourself whenever thoughts of bitterness begin to attack you. Your challenge is this: You must learn to resist negative thoughts before they hijack your emotions.

The enemy of our souls loves to taunt us with past failures, wrongs, disappointments, disasters, and calamities. And if we let him continue doing this, our life becomes a long and dark tunnel, with very little light at the end.

Charles Swindoll

Respecting Your Talents

Every good gift and every perfect gift is from above, and cometh down from the Father of lights.

James 1:17 KJV

Do you place a high value on your talents, your time, your capabilities, and your opportunities? If so, congratulations. But if you've acquired the insidious habit of devaluing your time, your work, or yourself, it's now time for a change.

Pearl Bailey correctly observed, "The first and worst of all frauds is to cheat one's self. All sin is easy after that."

If you've been squandering opportunities or selling yourself short, it's time to rethink the way that you think about yourself and your opportunities. No one can seize those opportunities for you, and no one can build up your self-confidence if you're unwilling to believe in yourself. So if you've been talking yourself down, stop. You deserve better. And if you don't give yourself healthy respect, who will?

Live the life you are given as well as you can.

Cardinal Joseph Bernadine

Your Growing Faith

I want you woven into a tapestry of love, in touch with everything there is to know of God. Then you will have minds confident and at rest, focused on Christ, God's great mystery.

Colossians 2:2 MSG

Your relationship with God is ongoing; it unfolds day by day, and it offers countless opportunities to grow closer to Him . . . or not. As each new day unfolds, you are confronted with a wide range of decisions: how you will behave, where you will direct your thoughts, with whom you will associate, and what you will choose to worship. These choices, along with many others like them, are yours and yours alone. How you choose determines how your relationship with God will unfold.

Are you continuing to grow in your love and knowledge of the Lord, or are you "satisfied" with the current state of your spiritual health? Hopefully, you're determined to make yourself a growing Christian. Your Savior deserves no less, and neither, by the way, do you.

Growing in any area of the Christian life takes time, and the key is daily sitting at the feet of Jesus.

Cynthia Heald

His Strength

The Lord is the strength of my life.

Psalm 27:1 KJV

Have you made God the cornerstone of your life, or is He relegated to a few hours on Sunday morning? Have you genuinely allowed God to reign over every corner of your heart, or have you attempted to place Him in a spiritual compartment? The answer to these questions will determine the direction of your day and your life.

God loves you. In times of trouble, He will comfort you; in times of sorrow, He will dry your tears. When you are weak or sorrowful, God is as near as your next breath. He stands at the door of your heart and waits. Welcome Him in and allow Him to rule. And then, accept the peace, and the strength, and the protection, and the abundance that only God can give.

He goes before us, follows behind us, and hems us safe inside the realm of His protection.

Beth Moore

Acceptance Now

People may make plans in their minds, but the Lord decides what they will do.

Proverbs 16:9 NCV

Sometimes, we must accept life on its terms, not our own. Life has a way of unfolding, not as we will, but as it will. And sometimes, there is precious little we can do to change things.

When events transpire that are beyond our control, we have a choice: we can either learn the art of acceptance, or we can make ourselves miserable as we struggle to change the unchangeable.

We must entrust the things we cannot change to God. Once we have done so, we can prayerfully and faithfully tackle the important work that He has placed before us: doing something about the things we can change . . . and doing it sooner rather than later.

Part of waiting upon the Lord is telling God that you want only what He wants—whatever it is.

Kay Arthur

Asking Him for Strength

Keep asking, and it will be given to you. Keep searching, and you will find. Keep knocking, and the door will be opened to you. For everyone who asks receives, and the one who searches finds, and to the one who knocks, the door will be opened.

Matthew 7:7-8 HCSB

If you need something, don't hesitate to ask God for His help. Are you in need of renewal? Ask God to strengthen you. Are you troubled? Take your concerns to Him in prayer. Are you discouraged? Seek the comfort of God's promises. Do you feel trapped in a life that lacks fulfillment and joy? Ask God where He wants you to go, and then go there. In all things great and small, seek the transforming power of God's grace. He hears your prayers, and He will answer.

God uses our most stumbling, faltering faith-steps as the open door to His doing for us "more than we ask or think."

Catherine Marshall

Counting Your Blessings

The Lord bless you and keep you; the Lord make His face shine upon you, and be gracious to you.

Numbers 6:24-25 NKJV

If you sat down and began counting your blessings, how long would it take? A very, very long time! Your blessings include life, freedom, family, friends, talents, and possessions, for starters. But, your greatest blessing—a gift that is yours for the asking—is God's gift of salvation through Christ Jesus.

Today, give thanks for your blessings by accepting them fully (with open arms) and by sharing them generously (with a thankful heart).

Billy Graham had this advice: "Think of the blessings we so easily take for granted: Life itself; preservation from danger; every bit of health we enjoy; every hour of liberty; the ability to see, to hear, to speak, to think, and to imagine all this comes from the hand of God." And that's sound advice for Christians—like you—who have been blessed beyond measure.

Jesus intended for us to be overwhelmed by the blessings of regular days. He said it was the reason he had come: "I am come that they might have life, and that they might have it more abundantly."

Gloria Gaither

The Rock

The Lord is my rock, my fortress, and my deliverer.

Psalm 18:2 HCSB

God is the Creator of life, the Sustainer of life, and the Rock upon which righteous lives are built. God is a never-ending source of support for those who trust Him, and He is a never-ending source of wisdom for those who study His Holy Word.

Is God the Rock upon which you've constructed your own life? If so, then you have chosen wisely. Your faith will give you the inner strength you need to rise above the inevitable demands and struggles of life.

Do the demands of this day seem overwhelming? If so, you must rely not only upon your own resources, but more importantly upon the Rock that cannot be shaken. God will hold your hand and walk with you today and every day if you let Him. Even if your circumstances are difficult, trust the Father. His promises remain true; His love is eternal; and His goodness endures. And because He is the One who can never be moved, you can stand firm in the knowledge that you are protected by Him now and forever.

He stands fast as your rock, steadfast as your safeguard, sleepless as your watcher, valiant as your champion.

C. H. Spurgeon

Accepting His Love

Praise the Lord, all nations! Glorify Him, all peoples! For great is His faithful love to us; the Lord's faithfulness endures forever. Hallelujah!

Psalm 117 HCSB

Because God's power is limitless, it is far beyond the comprehension of mortal minds. But even though we cannot fully understand the heart of God, we can be open to God's love.

God's ability to love is not burdened by temporal boundaries or by earthly limitations. The love that flows from the heart of God is infinite—and today presents yet another opportunity to celebrate that love.

You are a glorious creation, a unique individual, a beautiful example of God's handiwork. God's love for you is limitless. Accept that love, acknowledge it, and be grateful.

The life of faith is a daily exploration of the constant and countless ways in which God's grace and love are experienced.

Eugene Peterson

He Is with Us Always

I am not alone, because the Father is with Me.

John 16:32 HCSB

Where is God? God is eternally with us. He is omnipresent. He is, quite literally, everywhere you have ever been and everywhere you will ever go. He is with you night and day; He knows your every thought; He hears your every heartbeat.

Sometimes, in the crush of your daily duties, God may seem far away. Or sometimes, when the disappointments and sorrows of life leave you brokenhearted, God may seem distant, but He is not. When you earnestly seek God, you will find Him because He is here, waiting patiently for you to reach out to Him . . . right here . . . right now.

There is nothing more important in any life than the constantly enjoyed presence of the Lord. There is nothing more vital, for without it we shall make mistakes, and without it we shall be defeated.

Alan Redpath

God's Timing

Wait for the Lord; be courageous and let your heart be strong. Wait for the Lord.

Psalm 27:14 HCSB

We should learn to trust God's timing, but we are sorely tempted to do otherwise. Why? Because we human beings are usually anxious for things to happen sooner rather than later. But, God knows better.

God has created a world that unfolds according to His own timetable, not ours . . . thank goodness! We mortals might make a terrible mess of things. God does not. God's plan does not always happen in the way that we would like or at the time of our own choosing. Our task is to wait patiently and never lose hope.

In the words of Elisabeth Elliot, "We must learn to move according to the timetable of the Timeless One, and to be at peace." That's advice worth following today, tomorrow, and every day of your life.

Waiting on God brings us to the journey's end quicker than our feet.

Mrs. Charles E. Cowman

He Overcomes the World

God decided to let his people know this rich and glorious secret which he has for all people. This secret is Christ himself, who is in you. He is our only hope for glory.

Colossians 1:27 NCV

There are few sadder sights on earth than the sight of a person who has lost all hope. In difficult times, hope can be elusive, but Christians need never lose it. After all, God is good; His love endures; He has promised His children the gift of eternal life.

If you find yourself falling into the spiritual traps of worry and discouragement, consider the words of Jesus. It was Christ who promised, "In the world you will have tribulation; but be of good cheer, I have overcome the world" (John 16:33 NKJV). This world is, indeed, a place of trials and tribulations, but as believers, we are secure. God has promised us peace, joy, and eternal life. And, of course, God always keeps His promises.

I can still hardly believe it. I, with shriveled, bent fingers, atrophied muscles, gnarled knees, and no feeling from the shoulders down, will one day have a new body—light, bright and clothed in righteousness—powerful and dazzling.

Joni Eareckson Tada

Judging Others

Do not judge, or you too will be judged. For in the same way you judge others, you will be judged, and with the measure you use, it will be measured to you.

Matthew 7:1 NIV

We have all fallen short of God's commandments, and He has forgiven us. We, too, must forgive others. And, we must refrain from judging them.

Are you one of those people who finds it easy to judge others? If so, it's time to change.

God does not need (or, for that matter, want) your help. Why? Because God is perfectly capable of judging the human heart . . . while you are not.

As Christians, we are warned that to judge others is to invite fearful consequences: To the extent we judge others, so, too, will we be judged by God. Let us refrain, then, from judging our neighbors. Instead, let us forgive them and love them in the same way that God has forgiven us.

Perhaps the greatest blessing that religious inheritance can bestow is an open mind, one that can listen without judging.

Kathleen Norris

Looking for Miracles

Depend on the Lord and his strength; always go to him for help. Remember the miracles he has done; remember his wonders and his decisions.

Psalm 105:4-5 NCV

If you haven't seen any of God's miracles lately, you haven't been looking. Throughout history, the Creator has intervened in the course of human events in ways that cannot be explained by science or human rationale. And He's still doing so today.

God's miracles are not limited to special occasions, nor are they witnessed by a select few. God is crafting His wonders all around us: the miracle of the birth of a new baby, the miracle of a world renewing itself with every sunrise, the miracle of lives transformed by God's love and grace. Each day, God's handiwork is evident for all to see and experience.

Today, seize the opportunity to inspect God's hand at work. His miracles come in a variety of shapes and sizes, so keep your eyes and your heart open. Be watchful, and you'll soon be amazed.

Only God can move mountains, but faith and prayer can move God.

E. M. Bounds

When We Must Wait for God

Wait on the Lord, and He will rescue you.

Proverbs 20:22 HCSB

Life demands patience . . . and lots of it! We live in an imperfect world inhabited by imperfect people. Sometimes, we inherit troubles from others, and sometimes we create trouble for ourselves. In either case, what's required is patience.

Lamentations 3:25-26 reminds us that, "The Lord is wonderfully good to those who wait for him and seek him. So it is good to wait quietly for salvation from the Lord" (NIV). But, for most of us, waiting quietly for God is difficult. Why? Because we are fallible human beings, sometimes quick to anger and sometimes slow to forgive.

The next time you find your patience tested to the limit, remember that the world unfolds according to God's timetable, not ours. Sometimes, we must wait patiently, and that's as it should be. After all, think about how patient God has been with us.

In times of uncertainty, wait. Always, if you have any doubt, wait. Do not force yourself to any action. If you have a restraint in your spirit, wait until all is clear, and do not go against it.

Mrs. Charles E. Cowman

God Protects

I know whom I have believed, and am convinced that he is able to guard what I have entrusted to him for that day.

2 Timothy 1:12 NIV

God is willing to protect us. We, in turn, must open ourselves to His protection and His love. This point is illustrated by the familiar story found in the 4th chapter of Mark: When a terrible storm rose quickly on the Sea of Galilee, the disciples were afraid. Although they had witnessed many miracles, the disciples feared for their lives, so they turned to Jesus, and He calmed the waters and the wind.

Sometimes, we, like the disciples, feel threatened by the storms of life. And when we are fearful, we, too, can turn to Christ for comfort and for courage. The next time you find yourself facing a fear-provoking situation, remember that the One who calmed the wind and the waves is also your personal Savior. Then ask yourself which is stronger: your faith or your fear. The answer, friends, should be obvious: Whatever your challenge, God can handle it. Let Him.

Only believe, don't fear. Our Master, Jesus, always watches over us, and no matter what the persecution, Jesus will surely overcome it.

Lottie Moon

Forgiveness Is Liberating

Those who show mercy to others are happy, because God will show mercy to them.

Matthew 5:7 NCV

Bitterness is a form of self-punishment; forgiveness is a means of self-liberation. Bitterness focuses on the injustices of the past; forgiveness focuses on the blessings of the present and the opportunities of the future. Bitterness is an emotion that destroys you; forgiveness is a decision that empowers you. Bitterness is folly; forgiveness is wisdom.

If we call upon the Lord and seek to see the world through His eyes, He will give us guidance, wisdom and perspective. When we make God's priorities our priorities, He will lead us according to His plan and according to His commandments. When we study God's Word, we are reminded that God's reality is the ultimate reality. May we live—and forgive—accordingly.

As you have received the mercy of God by the forgiveness of sin and the promise of eternal life, thus you must show mercy.

Billy Graham

His Comforting Hand

When I am filled with cares, Your comfort brings me joy.

Psalm 94:19 HCSB

As Christians, we can be assured of this fact: Whether we find ourselves on the pinnacle of the mountain or in the darkest depths of the valley, God is there.

If you have been touched by the transforming hand of Jesus, then you have every reason to live courageously. After all, Christ has already won the ultimate battle—and He won it for you—on the cross at Calvary.

So the next time you find your courage tested to the limit, lean upon God's promises. Trust His Son. Remember that God is always near and that He is your protector and your deliverer. When you are worried, anxious, or afraid, call upon Him and accept the touch of His comforting hand. Remember that God rules both mountaintops and valleys—with limitless wisdom and love—now and forever.

When I am criticized, injured, or afraid, there is a Father who is ready to comfort me.

Max Lucado

Embraced by God

The unfailing love of the Lord never ends!

Lamentations 3:22 NLT

Every day of your life—indeed, every moment of your life—you are embraced by God. He is always with you, and His love for you is deeper and more profound than you can imagine. And now, precisely because you are a wondrous creation treasured by God, a question presents itself: What will you do in response to God's love? Will you ignore it or return it? Will you return it or neglect it? The decision, of course, is yours and yours alone.

When you open yourself to God's love, you feel differently about yourself, your neighbors, and your world. When you embrace God's love, you share His message and you obey His commandments.

When you accept the Father's grace and share His love, you are blessed here on earth and throughout all eternity. Accept His love today.

God will never let you be shaken or moved from your place near His heart.

Joni Eareckson Tada

Close to the Brokenhearted

I am the Lord who heals you.

Exodus 15:26 NCV

In time, tragedy visits all those who live long and love deeply. When our friends or family members encounter life-shattering events, we struggle to find words that might offer them comfort and support. But finding the right words can be difficult, if not impossible. Sometimes, all that we can do is to be with our loved ones and to pray for them, trusting that God will do the rest.

Thankfully, God promises that He is "close to the brokenhearted" (Psalm 34:18 NIV). In times of intense sadness, we must turn to Him, and we must encourage our friends and family members to do likewise. When we do so, our Father comforts us and, in time, He heals us.

One of the more significant things God will bring out of our grief and depression is an ability to walk constructively with others through theirs. In fact, one of the purposes of God's comfort is to equip us to comfort others.

David B. Biebel

Beyond Discouragement

The Lord is my light and my salvation; whom shall I fear? The Lord is the strength of my life; of whom shall I be afraid?

Psalm 27:1 NKJV

Because we are saved by a risen Christ, we can have hope for the future, no matter how desperate our circumstances may seem. After all, God has promised that we are His throughout eternity. And, He has told us that we must place our hopes in Him.

Today, summon the courage to follow God. Even if the path seems difficult, even if your heart is fearful, trust your Heavenly Father and follow Him. Trust Him with your day and your life. Do His work, care for His children, and share His Good News. Let Him guide your steps. He will not lead you astray.

If a person fears God, he or she has no reason to fear anything else. On the other hand, if a person does not fear God, then fear becomes a way of life.

Beth Moore

What Now, Lord?

For we are His making, created in Christ Jesus for good works, which God prepared ahead of time so that we should walk in them.

Ephesians 2:10 HCSB

God has things He wants you to do and places He wants you to go. The most important decision of your life is, of course, your commitment to accept Jesus Christ as your personal Lord and Savior. And, once your eternal destiny is secured, you will undoubtedly ask yourself the question, "What now, Lord?" If you earnestly seek God's will for your life, you will find it.

As you prayerfully consider God's path for your life, you should study His Word and be ever watchful for His signs. You should associate with fellow believers who will encourage your spiritual growth, and you should listen to that inner voice that speaks to you in the quiet moments of your daily devotionals.

Rest assured: God is here, and He intends to use you in wonderful, unexpected ways. He desires to lead you along a path of His choosing. Your challenge is to watch, to listen . . . and to follow.

Finding one's mission, and then fulfilling it, is perhaps the most vital activity in which a person can engage.

Laurie Beth Jones

Life Triumphant

Shout triumphantly to the Lord, all the earth. Serve the Lord with gladness; come before Him with joyful songs.

Psalm 100:1-2 HCSB

Are you living the triumphant life that God has promised? Or are you, instead, a spiritual shrinking violet? As you ponder that question, consider this: God does not intend that you live a life that is commonplace or mediocre. And He doesn't want you to hide your light "under a basket." Instead, He wants you to "Let your light so shine before men, that they may see your good works and glorify your Father in heaven" (Matthew 5:16 NKJV). In short, God wants you to live a triumphant life so that others might know precisely what it means to be a believer.

The Christian life should be a triumphal celebration, a daily exercise in thanksgiving and praise. Join that celebration today. And while you're at it, make sure that you let others know that you've joined.

The life of faith is a daily exploration of the constant and countless ways in which God's grace and love are experienced.

Eugene Peterson

Serving Others

Each one of us needs to look after the good of the people around us, asking ourselves, "How can I help?" That's exactly what Jesus did. He didn't make it easy for himself by avoiding people's troubles, but waded right in and helped out. "I took on the troubles of the troubled," is the way Scripture puts it.

Romans 15:2-3 MSG

How do you achieve greatness in the eyes of God? By making yourself a humble servant. Being a fallible human being, you may feel the temptation to build yourself up in the eyes of your neighbors. Resist that temptation. Instead, serve your neighbors quietly and without fanfare. Find a need and fill it humbly. Lend a helping hand and share a word of kindness anonymously. Take the time to minister to those in need.

Then, when you have done your best to serve your neighbors and to serve your God, you can rest comfortably knowing that in the eyes of your Heavenly Father, you have achieved greatness. And God's eyes, after all, are the only ones that really count.

Do things for others and you'll find your self-consciousness evaporating like morning dew on a Missouri cornfield in July.

Dale Carnegie

Defining Success

If you do not stand firm in your faith, then you will not stand at all.

Isaiah 7:9 HCSB

How do you define success? Do you define it as the accumulation of material possessions or the adulation of your neighbors? If so, you need to reorder your priorities. Genuine success has little to do with fame or fortune; it has everything to do with God's gift of love and His promise of salvation.

If you have accepted Christ as your personal Savior, you are already a towering success in the eyes of God, but there is still more that you can do. Your task—as a believer who has been touched by the Creator's grace—is to accept the spiritual abundance and peace that He offers through the person of His Son. Then, you can share the healing message of God's love and His abundance with a world that desperately needs both. When you do, you will have reached the pinnacle of success.

Nothing in this world is more fundamental for success in life than hope, and this star pointed to our only source of true hope: Jesus Christ.

D. James Kennedy

Each Day Is a Gift

Teach us to number our days carefully so that we may develop wisdom in our hearts.

Psalm 90:12 HCSB

This day is a gift from God. How will you use it? Will you celebrate God's gifts and obey His commandments? Will you share words of encouragement and hope with all who cross your path? Will you share the Good News of the risen Christ? Will you trust in the Father and praise His glorious handiwork? The answer to these questions will determine, to a surprising extent, the direction and the quality of your day.

The familiar words of Psalm 118:24 remind us of a profound yet simple truth: "This is the day which the LORD hath made; we will rejoice and be glad in it" (KJV). For Christian believers, every day begins and ends with God and His Son. Christ came to this earth to give us abundant life and eternal salvation. We give thanks to our Maker when we treasure each day and use it to the fullest.

Today, may we give thanks for this day and for the One who created it.

Live today fully, expressing gratitude for all you have been, all you are right now, and all you are becoming.

Melodie Beattie

Walking with God

How happy is everyone who fears the Lord, who walks in His ways!

Psalm 128:1 HCSB

Are you tired? Discouraged? Fearful? Be comforted. Take a walk with God. Jesus called upon believers to walk with Him, and He promised them that He would teach them how to live freely and lightly (Matthew 11:28-30). Are you worried or anxious? Be confident in God's power. He will never desert you. Do you see no hope for the future? Be courageous and call upon God. He will protect you and then use you according to His purposes. Are you grieving? Know that God hears your suffering. He will comfort you and, in time, He will dry your tears. Are you confused? Listen to the quiet voice of your Heavenly Father. He is not a God of confusion. Talk with Him; listen to Him; follow His commandments. He is steadfast, and He is your Protector . . . forever.

The man who walks with God always gets to his destination.

Henrietta Mears

Prayer and Work

Be kindly affectionate to one another with brotherly love, in honor giving preference to one another; not lagging in diligence, fervent in spirit, serving the Lord; rejoicing in hope, patient in tribulation, continuing steadfastly in prayer.

Romans 12:10-12 NKJV

The old adage is both familiar and true: We must pray as if everything depended upon God, but work as if everything depended upon us. Yet sometimes, when we are weary and discouraged, we may allow our worries to sap our energy and our hope. God has other intentions. God intends that we pray for things, and He intends that we be willing to work for the things that we pray for. More importantly, God intends that our work should become His work.

Are you willing to work diligently for yourself, for your family, and for your God? And are you willing to engage in work that is pleasing to your Creator? If so, you can expect Him to bring forth a rich harvest.

And if you have concerns about the inevitable challenges of everyday living, take those concerns to God in prayer. He will guide your steps, He will steady your hand, He will calm your fears, and He will reward your efforts.

A Heart Aflame?

Whatever work you do, do your best, because you are going to the grave, where there is no working . . . .

Ecclesiastes 9:10 NCV

We have every reason to be enthusiastic about life, but sometimes the struggles of daily living may cause us to feel decidedly unenthusiastic. Whenever we feel our energy begin to fade, it's time to slow down, to rest, to count our blessings, and to have a sensible talk with God. When we feel worried or weary, a few moments spent in quiet conversation with the Creator can calm our fears and restore our perspective.

Mary Lou Retton observed, "Heat is required to forge anything. Every great accomplishment is the story of a flaming heart." Is your heart aflame? Are you fully engaged in life—and in love? If so, keep up the good work! But if you feel the passion slowly draining from your life, it's time to refocus your thoughts, your energies, and your prayers . . . now.

Give me the love that leads the way, the faith that nothing can dismay, the hope no disappointments tire, the passion that will burn like fire. Let me not sink to be a clod: Make me thy fuel, flame of God.

Amy Carmichael

Happiness and Abundance

Happy are those who fear the Lord. Yes, happy are those who delight in doing what he commands.

Psalm 112:1 NLT

Do you seek happiness, abundance, and contentment? If so, here are some things you should do: Love God and His Son; depend upon God for strength; try, to the best of your abilities, to follow God's will; and strive to obey His Holy Word. When you do these things, you'll discover that happiness goes hand-in-hand with righteousness. The happiest people are not those who rebel against God; the happiest people are those who love God and obey His commandments.

What does life have in store for you? A world full of possibilities (of course it's up to you to seize them), and God's promise of abundance (of course it's up to you to accept it). So, as you embark upon the next phase of your journey, remember to celebrate the life that God has given you. Your Creator has blessed you beyond measure. Honor Him with your prayers, your words, your deeds, and your joy.

Christ is the secret, the source, the substance, the center, and the circumference of all true and lasting gladness.

Mrs. Charles E. Cowman

His Abundance

I have come that they may have life, and that they may have it more abundantly.

John 10:10 NKJV

The Bible gives us hope—as Christians we can enjoy lives filled with abundance.

But what, exactly, did Jesus mean when, in John 10:10, He promised "life . . . more abundantly"? Was He referring to material possessions or financial wealth? Hardly. Jesus offers a different kind of abundance: a spiritual richness that extends beyond the temporal boundaries of this world.

Is material abundance part of God's plan for our lives? Perhaps. But in every circumstance of life, during times of wealth or times of want, God will provide us what we need if we trust Him (Matthew 6). May we, as believers, claim the riches of Christ Jesus every day that we live, and may we share His blessings with all who cross our path.

It would be wrong to have a "poverty complex," for to think ourselves paupers is to deny either the King's riches or to deny our being His children.

Catherine Marshall

The Lessons of Tough Times

No discipline seems pleasant at the time, but painful. Later on, however, it produces a harvest of righteousness and peace for those who have been trained by it.

Hebrews 12:11 NIV

The times that try your soul are also the times that build your character. During the darker days of life, you can learn lessons that are impossible to learn during sunny, happier days. Times of adversity can—and should—be times of intense spiritual and personal growth. But God will not force you to learn the lessons of adversity. You must learn them for yourself.

The next time Old Man Trouble knocks on your door, remember that he has lessons to teach. So turn away Mr. Trouble as quickly as you can, but as you're doing so, don't forget to learn his lessons. And remember: the trouble with trouble isn't just the trouble it causes; it's also the trouble we cause ourselves if we ignore the things that trouble has to teach. Got that? Then please don't forget it!

A faith that hasn't been tested can't be trusted.

Adrian Rogers

Pray Without Ceasing

Anyone who is having troubles should pray.

James 5:13 NCV

In his first letter to the Thessalonians, Paul advised members of the new church to "pray without ceasing" (5:16-18). His advice applies to Christians of every generation. When we consult God on an hourly basis, we avail ourselves of His wisdom, His strength, and His love. As Corrie ten Boom observed, "Any concern that is too small to be turned into a prayer is too small to be made into a burden."

Today, instead of turning things over in your mind, turn them over to God in prayer. Instead of worrying about your next decision, ask God to lead the way. Don't limit your prayers to meals or bedtime. Pray constantly. God is listening, and He wants to hear from you.

For us the salve, the ointment that soothes the irritations of life, is Jesus Christ, the Great Physician. And we have instant communication with Him through times of prayerful solitude.

Franklin Graham

He Renews

Finally, be strengthened by the Lord and by His vast strength.

Ephesians 6:10 HCSB

God's Word is clear: When we genuinely lift our hearts and prayers to Him, He renews our strength. Are you almost too weary to lift your head? Then bow it. Offer your concerns and your fears to your Father in Heaven. He is always at your side, offering His love and His strength.

Are you troubled or anxious? Take your anxieties to God in prayer. Are you weak or worried? Delve deeply into God's Holy Word and sense His presence in the quiet moments of the early morning. Are you spiritually exhausted? Call upon fellow believers to support you, and call upon Christ to renew your spirit and your life. Your Savior will not let you down. To the contrary, He will lift you up when you ask Him to do so. So what, dear friend, are you waiting for?

Be still, and in the quiet moments, listen to the voice of your heavenly Father. His words can renew your spirit—no one knows you and your needs like He does.

Janet L. Weaver Smith

The Joy of Serving God

Shepherd God's flock, for whom you are responsible. Watch over them because you want to, not because you are forced. That is how God wants it. Do it because you are happy to serve.

1 Peter 5:2 NCV

Martha and Mary both loved Jesus, but they showed their love in different ways. Mary sat at the Master's feet, taking in every word. Martha, meanwhile, busied herself with preparations for the meal to come. When Martha asked Jesus if He was concerned about Mary's failure to help, Jesus replied, "Mary has chosen better" (Luke 10:42 NIV). The implication is clear: as believers, we must spend time with Jesus before we spend time for Him. But, once we have placed Christ where He belongs—at the center of our hearts—we must go about the business of serving the One who has saved us.

How can we serve Christ? By sharing His message and by serving those in need. As followers of Jesus, we must make ourselves humble servants to our families, to our neighbors, and to the world. We must help the helpless, love the unloved, protect the vulnerable, and care for the infirm. When we do, our lives will be blessed by the One who sacrificed His life for us.

Your Journey Continues

I've told you these things for a purpose: that my joy might be your joy, and your joy wholly mature.

John 15:11 MSG

Complete spiritual maturity is never achieved in a day, or in a year, or even in a lifetime. The journey toward spiritual maturity is an ongoing process that continues, day by day, throughout every stage of life. Every stage of life has its opportunities and its challenges, and if we're wise, we continue to seek God's guidance as each new chapter of life unfolds. Norman Vincent Peale advised: "Ask the God who made you to keep remaking you." That counsel is perfectly sound, but easy to ignore.

When we cease to grow, either emotionally or spiritually, we do ourselves a profound disservice. But, if we focus our thoughts—and attune our hearts—to the will of God, we will make each day another stage in the spiritual journey . . . and that's precisely what God intends for us to do.

You are either becoming more like Christ every day or you're becoming less like Him. There is no neutral position in the Lord.

Stormie Omartian

Thank Him Now

Our prayers for you are always spilling over into thanksgivings. We can't quit thanking God our Father and Jesus our Messiah for you!

Colossians 1:3 MSG

Sometimes, life can be complicated, demanding, and busy. When the demands of life leave us rushing from place to place with scarcely a moment to spare, we may fail to pause and say a word of thanks for all the good things we've received. But when we fail to count our blessings, we rob ourselves of the happiness, the peace, and the gratitude that should rightfully be ours.

Today, even if you're busily engaged in life, slow down long enough to start counting your blessings. You most certainly will not be able to count them all, but take a few moments to jot down as many blessings as you can. Then, give thanks to the Giver of all good things: God. His love for you is eternal, as are His gifts.

One reason why we don't thank God for his answer to our prayer is that frequently we don't recognize them as being answers to our prayers. We just take his bountiful supply or dramatic action for granted when it comes.

Evelyn Christenson

Beyond Our Obstacles

Even though good people may be bothered by trouble seven times, they are never defeated.

Proverbs 24:16 NCV

The occasional disappointments and failures of life are inevitable. Such setbacks are simply the price that we must occasionally pay for our willingness to take risks as we follow our dreams. But even when we encounter bitter disappointments, we must never lose faith.

The reassuring words of Hebrews 10:36 remind us that when we persevere, we will eventually receive that which God has promised. What's required is perseverance, not perfection.

When we encounter the inevitable difficulties of life, God stands ready to protect us. Our responsibility, of course, is to ask Him for protection. When we call upon Him in heartfelt prayer, He will answer—in His own time and according to His own plan—and He will heal us. And, while we are waiting for God's plans to unfold and for His healing touch to restore us, we can be comforted in the knowledge that our Creator can overcome any obstacle, even if we cannot.

If you learn from a defeat, you have not really lost.

Zig Ziglar

Forgiveness Now

Anyone who claims to live in God's light and hates a brother or sister is still in the dark.

1 John 2:9 MSG

Forgiveness is seldom easy, but it is always right. When we forgive those who have hurt us, we honor God by obeying His commandments. But when we harbor bitterness against others, we disobey God—with predictably unhappy results.

Are you easily frustrated by the inevitable shortcomings of others? Are you a prisoner of bitterness or regret? If so, perhaps you need a refresher course in the art of forgiveness.

If there exists even one person, alive or dead, whom you have not forgiven (and that includes yourself), follow God's commandment and His will for your life: forgive that person today. And remember that bitterness, anger, and regret are not part of God's plan for your life. Forgiveness is.

God calls upon the loved not just to love but to be loving. God calls upon the forgiven not just to forgive but to be forgiving.

Beth Moore

He Is Never Distant

Do not be afraid or discouraged. For the LORD your God is with you wherever you go.

Joshua 1:9 NLT

God is not a distant being. He is not absent from our world; to the contrary, God's hand is actively involved in the smallest details of our lives. God is not "out there"; He is "right here," continuously reshaping His creation.

God is with you always, listening to your thoughts and prayers, watching over your every move. As the demands of everyday life weigh down upon you, you may be tempted to ignore God's presence or—worse yet—to rebel against His commandments. But, when you quiet yourself and acknowledge His presence, God touches your heart and restores your spirit.

At this very moment, God is seeking to work in you and through you. So why not let Him do it right now?

A state of mind that sees God in everything is evidence of growth in grace and of a thankful heart.

Charles Finney

God Loves You

For God loved the world in this way: He gave His only Son, so that everyone who believes in Him will not perish but have eternal life.

John 3:16 HCSB

How much does God love you? To answer that question, you need only to look at the cross. God's love for you is so great that He sent His only Son to this earth to die for your sins and to offer you the priceless gift of eternal life.

You must decide whether or not to accept God's gift. Will you ignore it or embrace it? Will you return it or neglect it? Will you invite Christ to dwell in the center of your heart, or will you relegate Him to a position of lesser importance? The decision is yours, and so are the consequences. So choose wisely . . . and choose today.

Before anything else, above all else, beyond everything else, God loves us. God loves us extravagantly, ridiculously, without limit or condition. God is in love with us . . . God yearns for us.

Roberta Bondi

Infinite Possibilities

We know that all things work together for the good of those who love God: those who are called according to His purpose.

Romans 8:28 HCSB

Ours is a God of infinite possibilities. But sometimes, because of limited faith and limited understanding, we wrongly assume that God cannot or will not intervene in the affairs of mankind. Such assumptions are simply wrong.

Are you afraid to ask God to do big things in your life? Is your faith threadbare and worn? If so, it's time to abandon your doubts and reclaim your faith in God's promises.

God's Holy Word makes it clear: absolutely nothing is impossible for the Lord. And since the Bible means what it says, you can be comforted in the knowledge that the Creator of the universe can do miraculous things in your own life and in the lives of your loved ones. Your challenge, as a believer, is to take God at His word, and to expect the miraculous.

Think big, talk big, act big. Because we have a big God.

Kathryn Kuhlman

Impatient?

Therefore the Lord is waiting to show you mercy, and is rising up to show you compassion, for the Lord is a just God. Happy are all who wait patiently for Him.

Isaiah 30:18 HCSB

Most of us are impatient for God to grant us the desires of our heart. Usually, we know what we want, and we know precisely when we want it: right now, if not sooner. But God may have other plans. And when God's plans differ from our own, we must trust in His infinite wisdom and in His infinite love.

As busy people living in a fast-paced world, many of us find that waiting quietly for God is difficult. Why? Because we are fallible human beings seeking to live according to our own timetables, not God's. In our better moments, we realize that patience is not only a virtue, it is also a commandment from God.

God instructs us to be patient in all things. We must be patient with our families, our friends, and our associates. We must also be patient with our Creator as He unfolds His plan for our lives. And that's as it should be. Think how patient God has been with us.

The challenge before us is to have faith in God, and the hardest part of faith is waiting.

Jim Cymbala

The Peace of Christ

Peace, peace to you, and peace to him who helps you, for your God helps you.

1 Chronicles 12:18 HCSB

Through His Son, God offers a "peace that passes all understanding," but He does not force His peace upon us. God's peace is a blessing that we, as children of a loving Father, must claim for ourselves . . . but sometimes we are slow to do so. Why? Because we are fallible human beings with limited understanding and limited faith.

Have you found the lasting peace that can be yours through Jesus, or are you still rushing after the illusion of "peace and happiness" that the world promises but cannot deliver?

Today, as a gift to yourself, to your family, and to your friends, claim the inner peace that is your spiritual birthright: the peace of Jesus Christ. It is offered freely; it has been paid for in full; it is yours for the asking. So ask. And then share.

Where the soul is full of peace and joy, outward surroundings and circumstances are of comparatively little account.

Hannah Whitall Smiith

Living in Our Material World

A pretentious, showy life is an empty life; a plain and simple life is a full life.

Proverbs 13:7 MSG

On the grand stage of a well-lived life, material possessions should play a rather small role. Of course, we all need the basic necessities of life, but once we meet those needs for ourselves and for our families, the piling up of possessions creates more problems than it solves. Our real riches, of course, are not of this world. We are never really rich until we are rich in spirit.

Do you find yourself wrapped up in the concerns of the material world? If so, it's time to reorder your priorities by turning your thoughts and your prayers to more important matters. And, it's time to begin storing up riches that will endure throughout eternity: the spiritual kind.

We act as though comfort and luxury were the chief requirements of life, when all we need to make us really happy is something to be enthusiastic about.

Charles Kingsley

Trusting His Answers

Trust in the LORD with all your heart; do not depend on your own understanding.

Proverbs 3:5 NLT

God answers our prayers. What God does not do is this: He does not always answer our prayers as soon as we might like, and He does not always answer our prayers by saying "Yes." God isn't an order-taker, and He's not some sort of cosmic vending machine. Sometimes—even when we want something very badly—our loving Heavenly Father responds to our requests by saying "No," and we must accept His answer, even if we don't understand it.

God answers prayers not only according to our wishes but also according to His master plan. We cannot know that plan, but we can know the Planner . . . and we must trust His wisdom, His righteousness, and His love. Always.

All prayers are answered. We need to distinguish between a prayer unanswered and one not answered how or when we would like it to be.

Lloyd Ogilvie

The Merry-Go-Round

I will give you a new heart and put a new spirit within you.

Ezekiel 36:26 HCSB

For busy people living in a fast-paced, 21st-century world, life may seem like a merry-go-round that never stops turning. If that description seems to fit your life, then you may find yourself running short of patience, or strength, or both.

When you feel tired or discouraged, there is a source from which you can draw the power needed to recharge your spiritual batteries. That source is God.

Are you exhausted or troubled? Weak or worried? Worn out or burned out? If so, take time to rest, and take time to have a heart-to-heart talk with God. When you do, you'll discover that the Creator of the universe can help you gain a renewed sense of hope and a fresh perspective . . . your job is to let Him do it.

In those desperate times when we feel like we don't have an ounce of strength, He will gently pick up our heads so that our eyes can behold something—something that will keep His hope alive in us.

Kathy Troccoli

Your Own Worst Critic?

A devout life does bring wealth, but it's the rich simplicity of being yourself before God.

1 Timothy 6:6 MSG

Are you your own worst critic? If so, it's time to become a little more understanding of the person you see whenever you look into the mirror.

Millions of words have been written about various ways to improve self-image and increase self-esteem. Yet, maintaining a healthy self-image is, to a surprising extent, a matter of doing three things: 1. behaving ourselves 2. thinking healthy thoughts 3. finding a purpose for your life that pleases your Creator and yourself.

The Bible affirms the importance of self-acceptance by teaching Christians to love others as they love themselves (Matthew 22:37-40). God accepts us just as we are. And, if He accepts us—faults and all—then who are we to believe otherwise?

A healthy self-identity is seeing yourself as God sees you—no more and no less.

Josh McDowell

Spiritual Maturity

For this reason also, since the day we heard this, we haven't stopped praying for you. We are asking that you may be filled with the knowledge of His will in all wisdom and spiritual understanding.

Colossians 1:9 HCSB

The journey toward spiritual maturity lasts a lifetime: As Christians, we can and should continue to grow in the love and the knowledge of our Savior as long as we live. Norman Vincent Peale had simple advice for believers of all ages: "Ask the God who made you to keep remaking you." That advice, of course, is perfectly sound, but too often ignored.

When we cease to grow, either emotionally or spiritually, we do ourselves and our families a profound disservice. But, if we study God's Word, if we obey His commandments, and if we live in the center of His will, we will not be "stagnant" believers; we will, instead, be growing Christians . . . and that's exactly what God wants for our lives.

In those quiet moments when we open our hearts to God, the Creator who made us keeps remaking us. He gives us direction, perspective, wisdom, and courage. And, the appropriate moment to accept His spiritual gifts is always this one.

Beyond the Crises

But the wisdom that is from above is first pure, then peaceable, gentle, willing to yield, full of mercy and good fruits, without partiality and without hypocrisy.

James 3:17 NKJV

Your decision to seek a deeper relationship with God will not remove all problems from your life; to the contrary, it will bring about a series of personal crises as you constantly seek to say "yes" to God although the world encourages you to do otherwise. You live in a world that seeks to snare your attention and lead you away from God. Each time you are tempted to distance yourself from the Creator, you will face a spiritual crisis. A few of these crises may be monumental in scope, but most will be the small, everyday decisions of life. In fact, life here on earth can be seen as one test after another—and with each crisis comes yet another opportunity to grow closer to God . . . or to distance yourself from His plan for your life.

Today, you will face many opportunities to say "yes" to your Creator—and you will also encounter many opportunities to say "no" to Him. Your answers will determine the quality of your day and the direction of your life, so answer carefully . . . very carefully.

When Faith Slips Away

Immediately the father of the child cried out and said with tears, "Lord, I believe; help my unbelief!"

Mark 9:24 NKJV

Sometimes, like Jesus' disciples, we feel threatened by the storms of life. During these moments, when our hearts are flooded with uncertainty, we must remember that God is not simply near, He is here.

Have you ever felt your faith in God slipping away? If so, you are in good company. Even the most faithful Christians are, at times, beset by occasional bouts of discouragement and doubt. But even when you feel far removed from God, God never leaves your side. He is always with you, always willing to calm the storms of life. When you sincerely seek His presence—and when you genuinely seek to establish a deeper, more meaningful relationship with His Son—God will calm your fears, answer your prayers, and restore your soul.

We are most vulnerable to the piercing winds of doubt when we distance ourselves from the mission and fellowship to which Christ has called us.

Joni Eareckson Tada

God's Priceless Gift

Jesus said, "Everyone who drinks from this water will get thirsty again. But whoever drinks from the water that I will give him will never get thirsty again—ever! In fact, the water I will give him will become a well of water springing up within him for eternal life."

John 4:13-14 HCSB

Your ability to envision the future, like your life here on earth, is limited. God's vision, however, is not burdened by any such limitations. He sees all things, He knows all things, and His plans for you endure for all time.

God's plans are not limited to the events of life on earth. Your Heavenly Father has bigger things in mind for you . . . much bigger things. So praise the Creator for the gift of eternal life and share the Good News with all who cross your path. You have given your heart to the Son, so you belong to the Father—today, tomorrow, and for all eternity.

Jesus came down from heaven, revealing exactly what God is like, offering eternal life and a personal relationship with God, on the condition of our rebirth—a rebirth made possible through His own death on the cross.

Anne Graham Lotz

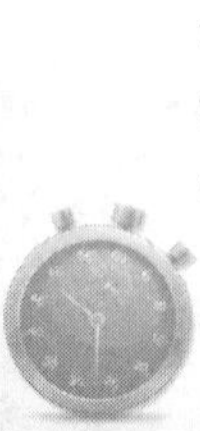

The Wisdom to Be Humble

Do you want to be counted wise, to build a reputation for wisdom? Here's what you do: Live well, live wisely, live humbly.

James 3:13 MSG

Humility is not, in most cases, a naturally occurring human trait. Most of us, it seems, are more than willing to overestimate our own accomplishments. We are tempted to say, "Look how wonderful I am!" . . . hoping all the while that the world will agree with our own self-appraisals. But those of us who fall prey to the sin of pride should beware—God is definitely not impressed by our prideful proclamations.

God honors humility . . . and He rewards those who humbly serve Him. So if you've acquired the wisdom to be humble, then you are to be congratulated. But if you've not yet overcome the tendency to overestimate your own accomplishments, then God still has some important (and perhaps painful) lessons to teach you—lessons about humility that you still need to learn.

A humble heart is like a magnet that draws the favor of God toward us.

Jim Cymbala

Depending upon God

Search for the Lord and for His strength; seek His face always.

Psalm 105:4-5 HCSB

God's love and support never changes. From the cradle to the grave, God has promised to give you the strength to meet any challenge. God has promised to lift you up and guide your steps if you let Him. God has promised that when you entrust your life to Him completely and without reservation, He will give you the courage to face any trial and the wisdom to live in His righteousness.

God's hand uplifts those who turn their hearts and prayers to Him. Will you count yourself among that number? Will you accept God's peace and wear God's armor against the temptations and distractions of our dangerous world? If you do, you can live courageously and optimistically, knowing that you have been forever touched by the loving, unfailing, uplifting hand of God.

When we reach the end of our strength, wisdom, and personal resources, we enter into the beginning of his glorious provisions.

Patsy Clairmont

Busy with Our Thoughts

People's thoughts can be like a deep well, but someone with understanding can find the wisdom there.

Proverbs 20:5 NCV

Because we are human, we are always busy with our thoughts. We simply can't help ourselves. Our brains never shut off, and even while we're sleeping, we mull things over in our minds. The question is not if we will think; the question is how will we think and what will we think about.

Today, focus your thoughts on God and His will. And if you've been plagued by pessimism and doubt, stop thinking like that! Place your faith in God and give thanks for His blessings. Think optimistically about your world and your life. It's the wise way to use your mind. And besides, since you will always be busy with your thoughts, you might as well make those thoughts pleasing (to God) and helpful (to you and yours).

No matter how little we can change about our circumstances, we always have a choice about our attitude toward the situation.

Vonette Bright

When Your Faith Is Tested

Blessed be the God and Father of our Lord Jesus Christ, the Father of mercies and the God of all comfort. He comforts us in all our affliction, so that we may be able to comfort those who are in any kind of affliction, through the comfort we ourselves receive from God.

2 Corinthians 1:3-4 HCSB

When the sun is shining and all is well, it is easy to have faith. But, when life takes an unexpected turn for the worse, as it will from time to time, your faith will be tested. In times of trouble and doubt, God remains faithful to you—and we must retain faith in yourself.

Social activist Jane Addams observed, "You do not know what life means when all the difficulties are removed. It's like eating a sweet dessert the first thing in the morning." And so it is with your own life.

So the next time you spot storm clouds on the horizon, remind yourself that every difficult day must come to an end . . . and when tough times are tough, tough people (like you) are tougher.

Let's thank God for allowing us to experience troubles that drive us closer to Him.

Shirley Dobson

Still Growing

When I was a child, I spoke and thought and reasoned as a child does. But when I grew up, I put away childish things.

1 Corinthians 13:11 NLT

God doesn't intend for any of us to be stagnate. Far from it! God's plan for us includes a lifetime of personal and spiritual growth—a lifetime of learning from our experiences . . . and sharing what we've learned.

We can and should continue to grow throughout every stage of life. But if we cease to grow, either emotionally or spiritually, we do ourselves and our loved ones a profound disservice.

It's a familiar saying, and it's true: "You aren't getting older, you're getting better!" And it's up to you to keep getting better every day that you live. When you do, you'll continue to shine your light upon a world that needs all the maturity and wisdom it can get.

People should think less about what they ought to do, and more about what they ought to be. If only their living were good, their work would shine forth brightly.

Meister Eckhart

Sharing the Joy

Let the hearts of those who seek the Lord rejoice. Look to the Lord and his strength; seek his face always.

1 Chronicles 16:10-11 NIV

God's intends that His joy should become our joy. He intends that we, His children, should share His love, His joy, and His peace. Yet sometimes, amid the inevitable hustle and bustle of daily life, we don't feel much like sharing. So we forfeit—albeit temporarily—God's joy as we wrestle with the challenges of everyday life.

If, today, your heart is heavy, open the door of your soul to your Heavenly Father. When you do, He will renew your spirit. And, if you already have the joy of Christ in your heart, share it freely. When you discover ways to make your joy become someone else's joy, you will have discovered a wonderful way to say, "I love you" to your family, to your friends, and, most especially, to your God.

To rejoice at another person's joy is like being in heaven.

Meister Eckhart

Walking in the Light

I have come as a light into the world, that whoever believes in Me should not abide in darkness.

John 12:46 NKJV

God's Holy Word instructs us that Jesus is, "the way, the truth, and the life" (John 14:6-7). Without Christ, we are as far removed from salvation as the east is removed from the west. And without Christ, we can never know the ultimate truth: God's truth.

Truth is God's way: He commands His believers to live in truth, and He rewards those who do so. Jesus is the personification of God's liberating truth, a truth that offers salvation to mankind.

Do you seek to walk with God? Do you seek to feel His presence and His peace? Then you must walk in truth; you must walk in the light; you must walk with the Savior. There is simply no other way.

If we do not radiate the light of Christ around us, the sense of the darkness that prevails in the world will increase.

Mother Teresa

Obedience Matters

Follow the whole instruction the Lord your God has commanded you, so that you may live, prosper, and have a long life in the land you will possess.

Deuteronomy 5:33 HCSB

Are you living outside the commandments of God? If so, you are inviting untold suffering into your own life and into the lives of your loved ones. God's commandments are not "suggestions," and they are not "helpful hints." They are, instead, immutable laws which, if followed, lead to repentance, salvation, and abundance. But if you disobey the commandments of your Heavenly Father or His Son, you will most surely reap a harvest of bitterness and regret.

Would you like a time-tested formula for successful living? Here is a formula that is proven and true: Study God's Word and obey it. Does this sound too simple? Perhaps it is simple, but it is also the only way to reap the marvelous riches that God has in store for you.

God asked both Noah and Joshua to do something unusual and difficult. They did it, and their obedience brought them deliverance.

Mary Morrison Suggs

The Plan for Your Life

The plans of hard-working people earn a profit, but those who act too quickly become poor.

Proverbs 21:5 NCV

Perhaps you have a clearly defined plan for the future, but even if you don't, rest assured that God does. God has a definite plan for every aspect of your life. Your challenge is straightforward: to sincerely pray for God's guidance, and to obediently follow the guidance you receive.

If you're burdened by the demands of everyday life here in the 21st century, you are not alone. Life is difficult at times, and uncertain. But of this you can be sure: God has a plan for you and yours. He will communicate His plans using the Holy Spirit, His Holy Word, and your own conscience. So listen to God's voice and be watchful for His signs: He will send you messages every day of your life, including this one. Your job is to listen, to learn, to trust, and to act.

Plan your work. Without a system, you'll feel swamped.

Norman Vincent Peale

During Difficult Days

In my trouble I called to the Lord; I cried out to my God. From his temple he heard my voice; my call for help reached his ears.

2 Samuel 22:7 NCV

All of us face difficult days. Sometimes even the most optimistic men and women can become discouraged, and you are no exception. If you find yourself enduring difficult circumstances, perhaps it's time for an extreme intellectual makeover—perhaps it's time to focus more on your strengths and opportunities, and less on the challenges that confront you. And one more thing: perhaps it's time to put a little more faith in God.

Your Heavenly Father is a God of possibility, not negativity. He will guide you through your difficulties and beyond them. And then, with a renewed spirit of optimism and hope, you can thank the Giver of all things good for gifts that are simply too numerous to count.

No matter how heavy the burden, daily strength is given, so I expect we need not give ourselves any concern as to what the outcome will be. We must simply go forward.

Annie Armstrong

Purpose Day by Day

Yet Lord, You are our Father; we are the clay, and You are our potter; we all are the work of Your hands.

Isaiah 64:8 HCSB

Each morning, as the sun rises in the east, you welcome a new day, one that is filled to the brim with opportunities, with possibilities, and with God. As you contemplate God's blessings in your own life, you should prayerfully seek His guidance for the day ahead.

Discovering God's unfolding purpose for your life is a daily journey, a journey guided by the teachings of God's Holy Word. As you reflect upon God's promises and upon the meaning that those promises hold for you, ask God to lead you throughout the coming day. Let your Heavenly Father direct your steps; concentrate on what God wants you to do now, and leave the distant future in hands that are far more capable than your own: His hands.

You're the only one who can do what you do.

Lois Evans

Beyond the Comfort Zone

Be not afraid, only believe.

Mark 5:36 KJV

Risk is an inevitable fact of life. From the moment we arise in the morning until the moment we drift off to sleep at night, we face a wide array of risks, both great and small.

Some risks, of course, should be avoided at all costs—these include risky behaviors that drive us farther and farther away from God's will for our lives. Yet other risks—the kinds of risks that we must take in order to expand our horizons and expand our faith—should be accepted as the inevitable price we must pay for living full and productive lives.

Have you planted yourself firmly inside your own comfort zone? If so, it's time to reconsider the direction and scope of your activities. God has big plans for you, but those plans will most likely require you to expand your comfort zone—or leave it altogether.

If I'm not free to fail, I'm not free to take risks. And everything in life that's worth doing involves a willingness to take a risk and involves the risk of failure. I have to try, but I do not have to succeed.

Madeleine L'Engle

Guard Your Heart

Guard your heart above all else, for it is the source of life.

Proverbs 4:23 HCSB

You are near and dear to God. He loves you more than you can imagine, and He wants the very best for you. And one more thing: God wants you to guard your heart.

Every day, you are faced with choices . . . lots of them. You can do the right thing, or not. You can tell the truth, or not. You can be kind, and generous, and obedient. Or not.

Today, the world will offer you countless opportunities to let down your guard and, by doing so, let the devil do his worst. Be watchful and obedient. Guard your heart by giving it to your Heavenly Father; it is safe with Him.

The fruit of our placing all things in God's hands is the presence of His abiding peace in our hearts.

Hannah Whitall Smith

What We Become

For it is God who is working among you both the willing and the working for His good purpose.

Philippians 2:13 HCSB

The old saying is both familiar and true: "What we are is God's gift to us; what we become is our gift to God." Each of us possesses special talents, gifted by God, that can be nurtured carefully or ignored totally. Our challenge, of course, is to use our abilities to the greatest extent possible and to use them in ways that honor our Savior.

Are you using your natural talents to make God's world a better place? If so, congratulations. But if you have gifts that you have not fully explored and developed, perhaps you need to have a chat with the One who gave you those gifts in the first place. Your talents are priceless treasures offered from your Heavenly Father. Use them. After all, an obvious way to say "thank you" to the Giver is to use the gifts He has given.

God often reveals His direction for our lives through the way He made us . . . with a certain personality and unique skills.

Bill Hybels

Whom Do You Trust?

The one who understands a matter finds success, and the one who trusts in the Lord will be happy.

Proverbs 16:20 HCSB

Where will you place your trust today? Will you trust in the ways of the world, or will you trust in the Word and the will of your Creator?

If you aspire to do great things for God's kingdom, you will trust Him completely.

Trusting God means trusting Him in every aspect of your life. You must trust Him with your relationships. You must trust Him with your finances. You must follow His commandments and pray for His guidance. Then, you can wait patiently for God's revelations and for His blessings.

When you trust your Heavenly Father without reservation, you can rest assured: in His own fashion and in His own time, God will bless you in ways that you never could have imagined. So trust Him, and then prepare yourself for the abundance and joy that will most certainly be yours through Him.

You will be able to trust Him only to the extent that you know Him!

Kay Arthur

Out of Balance?

Happy is the person who finds wisdom and gains understanding.

Proverbs 3:13 NLT

Sometimes, amid the concerns of everyday life, we lose perspective. Life seems out of balance as we confront an array of demands that sap our strength and cloud our thoughts. What's needed is a renewed faith, a fresh perspective, and God's wisdom.

Here in the 21st century, commentary is commonplace and information is everywhere. But the ultimate source of wisdom, the kind of timeless wisdom that God willingly shares with His children, is still available from a single unique source: the Holy Bible.

The wisdom of the world changes with the ever-shifting sands of public opinion. God's wisdom does not. His wisdom is eternal. It never changes. And it most certainly is the wisdom that you must use to plan your day, your life, and your eternal destiny.

He teaches us, not just to let us see ourselves correctly, but to help us see him correctly.

Kathy Troccoli

Worship Him

But an hour is coming, and is now here, when the true worshipers will worship the Father in spirit and truth. Yes, the Father wants such people to worship Him. God is Spirit, and those who worship Him must worship in spirit and truth.

John 4:23-24 HCSB

Where do we worship? In our hearts or in our church? The answer is both. As Christians who have been saved by a loving, compassionate Creator, we are compelled not only to worship the Creator in our hearts but also to worship Him in the presence of fellow believers.

We live in a world that is teeming with temptations and distractions—a world where good and evil struggle in a constant battle to win our hearts and souls. Our challenge, of course, is to ensure that we cast our lot on the side of God. One way to ensure that we do so is by the practice of regular, purposeful worship with our families. When we worship God faithfully and fervently, we are blessed.

Worship is about rekindling an ashen heart into a blazing fire.

Liz Curtis Higgs

Accepting the Past

I do not consider myself yet to have taken hold of it. But one thing I do: Forgetting what is behind and straining toward what is ahead, I press on toward the goal to win the prize for which God has called me heavenward in Christ Jesus.

Philippians 3:13-14 NIV

When you find the courage to accept the past by forgiving all those who have injured you (including yourself), you can then look to the future with a sense of optimism and hope.

Because we are saved by a risen Christ, we can have hope for the future, no matter how troublesome our circumstances may seem. After all, God has promised that we are His throughout eternity. And, He has told us that we must place our hopes in Him.

Of course, we will face disappointments and failures while we are here on earth, but these are only temporary defeats. Of course, this world can be a place of trials and tribulations, but we are secure. God has promised us peace, joy, and eternal life. And God keeps His promises today, tomorrow, and forever.

You cannot change the past, but you can control your own attitude.

Barbara Johnson

The Balancing Act

Come to Me, all you who labor and are heavy laden, and I will give you rest. Take My yoke upon you and learn from Me, for I am gentle and lowly in heart, and you will find rest for your souls. For My yoke is easy and My burden is light.

Matthew 11:28-30 NKJV

Face facts: life is a delicate balancing act, a tightrope walk with over-commitment on one side and under-commitment on the other. And it's up to each of us to walk carefully on that rope, not falling prey to pride (which causes us to attempt too much) or to fear (which causes us to attempt too little).

God's Word promises us the possibility of abundance (John 10:10). And we are far more likely to experience that abundance when we lead balanced lives.

Are you doing too much—or too little? If so, it's time to have a little chat with God. And if you listen carefully to His instructions, you will strive to achieve a more balanced life, a life that's right for you and your loved ones. When you do, everybody wins.

Every one of us is supposed to be a powerhouse for God, living in balance and harmony within and without.

Joyce Meyer

And the Greatest of These

Love is patient, love is kind and is not jealous; love does not brag and is not arrogant, does not act unbecomingly; it does not seek its own, is not provoked, does not take into account a wrong suffered, does not rejoice in unrighteousness, but rejoices with the truth; bears all things, believes all things, hopes all things, endures all things.

1 Corinthians 13:4-7 NASB

The beautiful words of 1st Corinthians 13 remind us that love is God's commandment: "But now abide faith, hope, love, these three; but the greatest of these is love" (v. 13, NASB). Faith is important, of course. So, too, is hope. But, love is more important still. Christ showed His love for us on the cross, and, as Christians, we are called upon to return Christ's love by sharing it. Today, let us spread Christ's love to families, friends, and strangers by word and by deed.

You can be sure you are abiding in Christ if you are able to have a Christlike love toward the people that irritate you the most.

Vonette Bright

About Anger

When you are angry, do not sin, and be sure to stop being angry before the end of the day. Do not give the devil a way to defeat you.

Ephesians 4:26-27 NCV

Sometimes, anger is appropriate. Even Jesus became angry when confronted with the moneychangers in the temple. On occasion, you, like Jesus, will confront evil, and when you do, you may respond as He did: vigorously and without reservation. But, more often than not, your frustrations will be of the more mundane variety.

As long as you live here on earth, you will face countless opportunities to lose your temper over small, relatively insignificant events: a traffic jam, a spilled cup of coffee, an inconsiderate comment, a broken promise. When you are tempted to lose your temper over the minor inconveniences of life, don't. Turn away from anger, hatred, bitterness, and regret. Turn instead to God.

Anger unresolved will only bring you woe.

Kay Arthur

God's Roadmap

Every word of God is flawless; he is a shield to those who take refuge in him.

Proverbs 30:5 NIV

God's Word is unlike any other book. The Bible is a roadmap for life here on earth and for life eternal. As Christians, we are called upon to study God's Holy Word, to trust its promises, to follow its commandments, and to share its Good News with the world.

As believers who seek to follow in the footsteps of the One from Galilee, we must study the Bible and meditate upon its meaning for our lives. Otherwise, we deprive ourselves of a priceless gift from our Creator. God's Holy Word is, indeed, a transforming, life-changing, one-of-a-kind treasure. And, a passing acquaintance with the Good Book is insufficient for Christians who seek to obey God's Word and to understand His will.

I believe the Bible is the best gift God has ever given to men. All the good from the Savior of the world is communicated to us through this book.

Abraham Lincoln

Actions Speak Louder

Are there those among you who are truly wise and understanding? Then they should show it by living right and doing good things with a gentleness that comes from wisdom.

James 3:13 NCV

The old saying is both familiar and true: actions speak louder than words. And as believers, we must beware: our actions should always give credence to the changes that Christ can make in the lives of those who walk with Him.

God calls upon each of us to act in accordance with His will and with respect for His commandments. If we are to be responsible believers, we must realize that it is never enough simply to hear the instructions of God; we must also live by them. And it is never enough to wait idly by while others do God's work here on earth; we, too, must act. Doing God's work is a responsibility that each of us must bear, and when we do, our loving Heavenly Father rewards our efforts with a bountiful harvest.

What we practice, not (save at rare intervals) what we preach, is usually our great contribution to the conversion of others.

C. S. Lewis

What's Your Attitude?

Set your minds on what is above, not on what is on the earth.

Colossians 3:2 HCSB

What's your attitude today? Are you fearful, angry, bored, or worried? Are you worried more about pleasing your friends than about pleasing your God? Are you confused, bitter, or pessimistic? If so, God wants to have a little talk with you.

God created you in His own image, and He wants you to experience joy and abundance. But, God will not force His joy upon you; you must claim it for yourself. So today, and every day thereafter, celebrate this life that God has given you. Think optimistically about yourself and your future. Give thanks to the One who has given you everything, and trust in your heart that He wants to give you so much more.

You've heard the saying, "Life is what you make it." That means we have a choice. We can choose to have a life full of frustration and fear, but we can just as easily choose one of joy and contentment.

Dennis Swanberg

Too Busy

Don't burn out; keep yourselves fueled and aflame. Be alert servants of the Master, cheerfully expectant. Don't quit in hard times; pray all the harder.

Romans 12:11-12 MSG

Has the busy pace of life robbed you of the peace that might otherwise be yours through Jesus Christ? If so, you are simply too busy for your own good. Through His Son Jesus, God offers you a peace that passes human understanding, but He won't force His peace upon you; in order to experience it, you must slow down long enough to sense His presence and His love.

Today, as a gift to yourself, to your family, and to the world, slow down and claim the inner peace that is your spiritual birthright: the peace of Jesus Christ. It is offered freely; it has been paid for in full; it is yours for the asking. So ask. And then share.

Getting things accomplished isn't nearly as important as taking time for love.

Janette Oke

Making Quality Choices

I am offering you life or death, blessings or curses. Now, choose life! . . . To choose life is to love the Lord your God, obey him, and stay close to him.

Deuteronomy 30:19-20 NCV

Every life, including yours, is a tapestry of choices. And the quality of your life depends, to a surprising extent, on the quality of the choices you make.

Would you like to enjoy a life of abundance and significance? If so, you must make choices that are pleasing to God.

From the instant you wake up in the morning until the moment you nod off to sleep at night, you make lots of decisions: decisions about the things you do, decisions about the words you speak, and decisions about the thoughts you choose to think.

Today and every day, it's up to you (and only you) to make wise choices, choices that enhance your relationship with God. After all, He deserves no less than your best.

Every day, I find countless opportunities to decide whether I will obey God and demonstrate my love for Him or try to please myself or the world system. God is waiting for my choices.

Bill Bright

Courtesy Matters

Be hospitable to one another without grumbling.

1 Peter 4:9 NKJV

Did Christ instruct us in matters of etiquette and courtesy? Of course He did. Christ's instructions are clear: "In everything, therefore, treat people the same way you want them to treat you, for this is the Law and the Prophets" (Matthew 7:12 NASB). Jesus did not say, "In some things, treat people as you wish to be treated." And, He did not say, "From time to time, treat others with kindness." Christ said that we should treat others as we wish to be treated in every aspect of our daily lives. This, of course, is a tall order indeed, but as Christians, we are commanded to do our best.

Today, be a little kinder than necessary to family members, friends, and total strangers. And, as you consider all the things that Christ has done in your life, honor Him with your words and with your deeds.

Reach out and care for someone who needs the touch of hospitality. The time you spend caring today will be a love gift that will blossom into the fresh joy of God's Spirit in the future.

Emilie Barnes

Beyond Your Hardships

He gives power to the weak, and to those who have no might He increases strength.

Isaiah 40:29 NKJV

We Christians have many reasons to celebrate. God is in His heaven; Christ has risen, and we are the sheep of His flock. Yet sometimes, even the most devout Christians can become discouraged. After all, we live in a world where expectations can be high and demands can be even higher. If you become discouraged with the direction of your day or your life, turn your thoughts and prayers to God. He is a God of possibility, not negativity. He will help you count your blessings instead of your hardships. And then, with a renewed spirit of optimism and hope, you can properly thank your Father in heaven for His blessings, for His love, and for His Son.

Just as courage is faith in good, so discouragement is faith in evil, and, while courage opens the door to good, discouragement opens it to evil.

Hannah Whitall Smith

Beyond Envy

Let us not become boastful, challenging one another, envying one another.

Galatians 5:26 NASB

Because we are frail, imperfect human beings, we are sometimes envious of others. But God's Word warns us that envy is sin. Thus, we must guard ourselves against the natural tendency to feel resentment and jealousy when other people experience good fortune.

As believers, we have absolutely no reason to be envious of any people on earth. After all, as Christians we are already recipients of the greatest gift in all creation: God's grace. We have been promised the gift of eternal life through God's only begotten Son, and we must count that gift as our most precious possession.

Rather than succumbing to the sin of envy, we should focus on the marvelous things that God has done for us—starting with Christ's sacrifice. And we must refrain from preoccupying ourselves with the blessings that God has chosen to give others.

So here's a surefire formula for a happier, healthier life: Count your own blessings and let your neighbors count theirs. It's the godly way to live.

Discontent dries up the soul.

Elisabeth Elliot

Actions Speak Louder

Because the kingdom of God is present not in talk but in power.

1 Corinthians 4:20 NCV

Our words speak, but our actions speak much more loudly. And whether we like it or not, all of us are role models. Since our friends and family members observe our actions, we are obliged to act in ways that demonstrate what it means to be a follower of Christ. As the old saying goes, "It's good to be saved and know it. But it's even better to be saved and show it!"

Today, make this promise to your God and to yourself: promise to be the kind of role model that honors your Heavenly Father and His only begotten Son. When you do so, you will be an ambassador for Christ and a positive role model to a world that needs both.

Be sure that you first preach by the way you live. If you do not, people will notice that you say one thing, but live otherwise, and your words will bring only cynical laughter and a derisive shake of the head.

Charles Cardinal Borromeo

Share His Joy

The Lord reigns; let the earth rejoice.

Psalm 97:1 NKJV

The Lord intends that believers should share His love with His joy in their hearts. Yet sometimes, amid the inevitable hustle and bustle of life, we can forfeit—albeit temporarily—God's joy as we wrestle with the challenges of daily living.

Joni Eareckson Tada spoke for Christians of every generation when she observed, "I wanted the deepest part of me to vibrate with that ancient yet familiar longing, that desire for something that would fill and overflow my soul."

If, today, your heart is heavy, open the door of your soul to Christ. He will give you peace and joy. And if you already have the joy of Christ in your heart, share it freely, just as Christ freely shared His joy with you.

Joy is the characteristic by which God uses us to remake the distressing into the desired, the discarded into the creative. Joy is prayer—joy is strength—joy is love—joy is a net of love by which you can catch souls.

Mother Teresa

Accepting Christ

We know very well that we are not set right with God by rule-keeping but only through personal faith in Jesus Christ.

Galatians 2:16 MSG

God's love for you is deeper and more profound than you can imagine. God's love for you is so great that He sent His only Son to this earth to die for your sins and to offer you the priceless gift of eternal life. Now, you must decide whether or not to accept God's gift. Will you ignore it or embrace it? Will you return it or neglect it? Will you accept Christ, or will you turn from Him?

Your decision to accept Christ is the pivotal decision of your life. It is a decision that you cannot ignore. It is a decision that is yours and yours alone. It is a decision with profound consequences, both earthly and eternal. Accept God's gift: Accept Christ today.

Surrender to the Lord is not a tremendous sacrifice, not an agonizing performance. It is the most sensible thing you can do.

Corrie ten Boom

God's Gift to You

Everything God made is good, and nothing should be refused if it is accepted with thanks.

1 Timothy 4:4 NCV

Life is God's gift to you, and He intends that you celebrate His glorious gift. If you're a Christian who treasures each day, you will be blessed by God.

For thoughtful believers, every day begins and ends with God and His Son. Christ came to this earth to give us abundant life and eternal salvation. Our task is to accept Christ's grace with joy in our hearts and praise on our lips. Believers who fashion their days around Jesus are transformed: They see the world differently, they act differently, and they feel differently about themselves and their neighbors.

So whatever this day holds for you, begin it and end it with God as your partner and Christ as your Savior. And throughout the day, give thanks to the One who created you and saved you. God's love for you is infinite. Accept it joyously and be thankful.

Shout the shout of faith. Nothing can withstand the triumphant faith that links itself to omnipotence. For "this is the victory that overcometh the world." The secret of all successful living lies in this shout of faith.

Hannah Whitall Smith

When Courage Is Tested

Be strong and courageous, all you who put your hope in the Lord.

Psalm 31:24 HCSB

Even the most dedicated Christians can find their courage tested by the inevitable disappointments and tragedies of life. After all, we live in a world filled with uncertainty, hardship, sickness, and danger. Old Man Trouble, it seems, is never too far from the front door.

When we focus upon our fears and our doubts, we may find many reasons to lie awake at night and fret about the uncertainties of the coming day. A better strategy, of course, is to focus not upon our fears, but instead upon our God.

God is as near as your next breath, and He is in control. He offers salvation to all His children, including you. God is your shield and your strength; you are His forever. So don't focus your thoughts upon the fears of the day. Instead, trust God's plan and His eternal love for you. And remember: whatever the size of your challenge, God is bigger.

I have found the perfect antidote for fear. Whenever it sticks up its ugly face, I clobber it with prayer.

Dale Evans Rogers

The Great Commission

Go, therefore, and make disciples of all nations, baptizing them in the name of the Father and of the Son and of the Holy Spirit, teaching them to observe everything I have commanded you. And remember, I am with you always, to the end of the age.

Matthew 28:19-20 HCSB

Are you a bashful Christian, one who is afraid to speak up for your Savior? Do you leave it up to others to share their testimonies while you stand on the sidelines, reluctant to share yours? Too many of us are slow to obey the last commandment of the risen Christ; we don't do our best to "make disciples of all the nations."

Christ's Great Commission applies to Christians of every generation, including our own. As believers, we are commanded to share the Good News with our families, with our neighbors, and with the world. Jesus invited His disciples to become fishers of men. We, too, must accept the Savior's invitation, and we must do so today. Tomorrow may indeed be too late.

Our commission is quite specific. We are told to be His witness to all nations. For us, as His disciples, to refuse any part of this commission frustrates the love of Jesus Christ, the Son of God.

Catherine Marshall

Don't burn out; keep yourselves
fueled and aflame.
Be alert servants of the Master,
cheerfully expectant.
Don't quit in hard times; pray all the harder.

—

Romans 12:11-12 MSG

How busy we have become . . .
and as a result, how empty!

—

Charles Swindoll